FOUR WHEELS
TO A
FORTUNE

SEVENTH EDITION

FOUR WHEELS TO A FORTUNE

This book represents the personal views of the author based on his own experiences gained within the motor trade and generally. Other people may well come to different views and conclusions. Every care has been taken by the author to fairly reflect not only accuracy but also fair objective opinion. No person should rely wholly upon any statements or conclusions contained in this work and, if purchasing or selling a motor vehicle, should rely on such further advice as may be appropriate. Save as required by law, no liability will be accepted by the author or publisher for any part of the content of this book, nor shall they be liable for any damage to any person or their property or loss arising from such person acting on the contents of or the information or views expressed in this book. It must be remembered and borne in mind that each vehicle must be viewed and judged upon its own individual condition, especially as regards roadworthiness, safety and commercial factors generally. No book of a general nature such as this can be taken to relate to or apply to each and every individual vehicle which the reader may be concerned with.

1st Edition 1986
2nd Edition 1987
3rd Edition 1987
4th Edition 1988
5th Edition 1989
6th Edition 1995
7th Edition 2001

© 1986, 1987, 1988, 1989, 1995, 2001 CM Cust

SEVENTH EDITION

ISBN 0 9513293 7 5

Written by CM Cust
Published by Charterhouse Books Limited, Exeter
Typeset by Exe Print, Exeter
Printed and bound by Exe Print, Exeter
Cartoons by Paul Sample

CONTENTS

PART I

PART II

ILLUSTRATIONS

by Paul Sample

'If a man takes with him a mind full of wisdom he can carry nothing better;
riches like this on a strange road will do more good than gold.'
From the ancient Viking poem "Hávamál" circa 700 AD

GLOSSARY OF DEALERS' SLANG

Ticket	M.O.T.
Pudding	Body filler
Dog	Rough car
Kettle	Car that boils
Toffee apple	Car superficially smart but rotten inside
Tart	Car badly prepared for sale
Landmark/Shed	Car that won't sell
Lemon	Car not to be bought at any price
World tourer	High mileage car
Cuckoo/Haircut	Clocked car/the act of clocking
Carbuncle	Old/experienced car dealer
Smoker	Dealer's own car
Shrapnel	Bangers/old cars
Boots	Tyres
Hum in the bum	Axle whine
Camy	Noisy camshaft
Endy	Rattling big or small end bearings
Boxy	Noisy gearbox
Shout/Tickle	Profit
Punter	Potential buyer
Pitch	Dealer's garage/premises
Rag it	Advertise car in newspaper
Wad	Money
Minter	Car in mint condition
Tosh up	Clean up a car
The drip	HP/Lease agreement

FOREWORD

Welcome to the world of motor trading! And a fascinating world it is! As motor trading is as large a subject as life itself, and I realise that people will wish to enter the business at different levels because their individual experience, means and motivation vary, I have divided the book into two parts.

Part I is designed to offer the reader an appreciation of how it is possible to enter the motor trade on the bottom rung – as, indeed, I did myself with virtually no money at all – and then, simply through diligence and common sense, work quite quickly up the ladder as both finances and experience accumulate.

Part II is more concerned with conventional and established retail motor trading and therefore will provide some helpful hints to those who have either worked their way up to this position or who are fortunate enough to have the capital and backing to go straight in at this level. However, never lose sight of the fact that some of the largest fortunes in motor trading have been made by those who have started out as 'banger men'!

Because, inevitably, there is a cross-over of information between both parts of the book, I would strongly advise all readers to start at the beginning and read it right the way through. I am conscious of the fact that for every reader who has serious intentions with regard to becoming involved in motor trading, there are many more who simply wish to read this book out of curiosity, which is fine by me. Motor trading is a serious subject but it does lend itself to lighter moments, so I hope that I have succeeded in presenting an accurate but lighthearted overview of the business.

PART I

CHAPTER ONE

GETTING STARTED

The most difficult period in a business career is when getting started and established in the first place. This is the time one is most likely to make mistakes but least able to afford them. Motor dealing is certainly no exception, which is why this part of the book places considerable emphasis on trying to help the beginner over the first hurdles by pointing out many of the pitfalls and demonstrating how to minimise financial risks in the early stages.

Many business advice publications appear to assume that the reader must be in possession of a substantial amount of capital even to consider going into this line of business in the first place. I have based Part I of this book on the opposite assumption, which is that most readers have probably got only a few hundred pounds available to dabble with. Having started with £150 myself, no-one is in a better position to appreciate just how much difference there is in starting out with a few hundred pounds or starting out with tens of thousands.

Although car design has moved on in leaps and bounds since I first started out some ten years ago, and although the model range of each manufacturer has expanded beyond belief during that time, the principles outlined here are basically exactly the same today as they were then, and indeed, the capital injection required is no greater. In fact, ironically, in real terms it could be argued that the cars are even cheaper today, especially after this recent recession which has had a dramatic effect on the overall value structure of used cars.

What I hope to demonstrate here is that by adopting a certain approach to motor dealing, it is possible to become established and successful quite quickly, in a matter of one or two years, without the need for large capital injection in the early stages. Realistically, there is only one way of entering motor trading in order to achieve this, and it will therefore be this method which I shall be recommending as the best way to start. As I explain it, I hope to show that there are also other advantages for the beginner in adopting this approach.

Before I begin to explain what this method is, I should like to run quickly over some points concerning motor dealing generally in order to explain how I arrived at the conclusion that this is indeed the best way to get into the business as a beginner with limited funds.

HOW MOST PEOPLE START

What the average potential motor trader with limited capital does to get himself started in the business is to attend local auctions, buy cheap bangers, 'the shrapnel', as they are known in the trade, and then sell them to the public through newspaper adverts. After a few years of this, if he has kept some books, he may be able to persuade a bank to loan him enough to buy or lease his own pitch, or perhaps enter into some kind of partnership with another trader. This is a slow and painful climb, and I can only say that in my experience of watching other people struggling to do it, I wouldn't recommend it to anyone.

Buying bangers from auctions and selling them to the public is a dangerous game nowadays. With the Department of Fair Trading and other 'consumer rights' bodies to back him up, Joe Public has everything on his side. No matter how well-intentioned you might be in setting out to supply what you consider as being reasonable cars for reasonable prices, if you unwittingly sell a bad car, you will discover that the motor dealer is usually regarded as the villain of the piece today; he seldom gets the benefit of the doubt. Don't misunderstand me, there is nothing particularly wrong with buying more expensive cars from auction which are warranted 'as good' because with these you get a chance to test them and normally have up until one hour after the sale ends to reject them or negotiate a rebate (a 'knock') to cover any defective aspect which you have discovered. Buying bangers sold 'as seen', however, is like playing Russian roulette. For a start, however experienced you may be mechanically, you can never be absolutely certain that you will not get caught with a 'lemon' simply because you can't test the car properly. Secondly, and more importantly, nowadays if you sell a car to the public, it is one hundred per cent your responsibility to make it roadworthy. Some people mistakenly believe that if they buy a car at auction with an MOT Certificate, should anything subsequently prove to be wrong with it, they can pass the buck to the MOT Station. This is not so. Even if the MOT Certificate is brand new, and the issuing MOT Station is proved to be at fault, you may still be prosecuted if the car is dangerously unroadworthy because it is your responsibility to put it right before selling it on.

Bear in mind also that any car sold 'as seen' under auction rules does not have to be in roadworthy condition, so it is no use trying to pass the buck back to the auctioneers either; they are protected by law. The point is, it is easy enough for the inexperienced to unwittingly sell a car in an unroadworthy condition. Unfortunately, however, ignorance is no refuge from the law.

Apart from these considerations, there is the practical aspect that it is very difficult to make a sure, regular living from selling cars like this. There will always be bad patches as well as good. In the bad periods, you will either find that you cannot purchase enough good cars at the right price, or simply shift the ones that you have; often this is for seasonal reasons. Unless you have enough spare cash to tide you over the bad times, it is difficult to build and accumulate capital fast enough to get ahead this way. All in all, this is not a professional approach to the whole matter.

THE BEST WAY TO START

I believe that the quickest, easiest and safest way of making money out of cars, particularly in the early stages, is not, in fact, to sell them to the public at all, but to go for maximum turnover by becoming a trade dealer. A trade dealer simply buys and sells cars purely within the motor trade itself; either by buying cars from the trade and selling them at auction, or indeed, buying and selling cars between auctions. Most trade dealing, however, involves buying cars from one dealer and selling to another.

I am convinced that it is more difficult to get started in the motor business in these highly competitive days through normal retailing than it is through trade dealing. Consider these practical aspects: to be a successful retailer, you have to hold a wide range of cars in stock, which brings us back to the old problem of capital. In the case of trade dealing, you need only a fraction of the capital necessary for retailing, because you are making money by turning over cars quickly. In fact, once you have established a reputation in the business, a large proportion of your transactions between dealers can be done on a 'sale or return' basis, in which case, it is seldom necessary to actually purchase these cars at all.

Every time a trade dealer sells a car, he makes a quick, sure profit and gets his capital back straightaway to put into another one, whereas in retailing, the capital can be frozen in a particular vehicle for months. Theoretically, the retail profit margin should cover this but increasingly today, margins are narrowing due to the pressure of competition. Added to which, run-of-the-mill cars depreciate in value all the time, so every month a car sits on a forecourt, it is not only worth a little less but also the cost of borrowing the capital tied up in that vehicle has eaten into the profit margin that little bit more.

Obviously, once you have accumulated experience and capital through trade dealing, you can always then branch out into whatever aspect of motor dealing interests you the most. This book has sections covering most other aspects of the business which may be of help when that time comes. Success in this business, as in any other, depends entirely on how much effort is put into it but the potential rewards can be high relative to that effort. It is obviously impractical for me to offer a tailor-made system which will work for every individual but what I can do is pass on the benefit of hard-earned experience. After that, your own input in terms of initiative and resourcefulness will ultimately determine your success.

CHAPTER TWO

How To Become A Trade Dealer

Setting yourself up as a trade dealer does require a little nerve at first but almost certainly not as much as you will imagine. Basically, it involves calling in at the main garages in your area and asking them if they have any cars recently traded in against newer ones, which they wish to dispose of or 'trade off' as it is known in the trade.

Larger garages 'trade off' cars for two main reasons: firstly, they normally have a policy concerning the age of vehicles they retail. Usually, for reasons of image, they will not retail cars over four years old unless they are exceptional, or, for instance, have classic or collectable status. Secondly, many garages only deal in specific makes like Renault or Ford, and therefore most cars of other makes which they take in part exchange are automatically disposed of through the trade; this is where you come in.

You could be forgiven for imagining that to stroll into a garage off the street and declare yourself to be a trader will require you to produce some kind of proof or business credentials. In fact, it is extremely rare that you will ever be asked to do so and in fact, in my experience, I cannot recall ever being challenged by any of the hundreds of garages I have approached. However, if this aspect worries you, then it is no big deal simply to have business cards made up by your local 'Quick Print' type shop. Indeed, a card like this can prove extremely useful when negotiating trade discounts for spare parts and other benefits which I shall be going into in a later chapter. All a business card basically has to state is something like *Joe Bloggs, Trade Buyer* and include a phone number.

Undoubtedly, the thing which will surprise you the most at

first is that garages will prove remarkably reasonable to deal with when you approach them like this and they will usually demonstrate a surprising amount of ready trust in terms of allowing you to take cars for test runs and so forth. Also, for the main part, in my experience they will be remarkably frank about the rights and wrongs of any particular vehicle you are looking at. You see, people who deal in cars all the time come to accept the fact that very few cars are completely fault free, including new ones for that matter! It is this pragmatic view of the motoring world which really separates the professionals from the amateurs.

When you are considering any particular vehicle, it is up to you to decide how much any particular problem matters. For instance, if it is a safety related fault, like defective brakes, then your conscience should demand that you put it right, in which case you will not buy the car unless the garage concerned is prepared to make an allowance to cover this. If the problem, however, is a less serious one, perhaps a little 'hum in the bum' when test driving, then this will not affect your profit margin when you sell the car at auction. Of course, if you were retailing the car, then you would have to spend time and money putting this right but providing you are intending to put it under the hammer 'as seen', you are protected by law from comeback. Any prospective purchaser of this vehicle knows that he or she is taking a risk buying a vehicle at auction, and therefore must accept that in order to get a bargain, it will be necessary to put problems like this right at some stage. It is a very foolish person who goes to auction without making allowance for extra expenses of this nature.

One of the many advantages of trade buying is that, because you can actually test the cars properly and sometimes even get a chance to put them on a ramp or over a pit, it is usually the safest way of buying bargains. Cars can almost always be bought cheaper from the trade than they can at auction. One does not have to ponder long on the economics of the motor trade to work out why this is. Busy garages cannot spare the time or personnel to take all of their trade-in vehicles to auction. For instance, if one of their mechanics is sent down to the auction, he can only drive one car there and then he will probably have to wait three or four hours for it to sell. Four hours of a mechanic's time is too great a sacrifice for most garages, especially as their service departments are usually booked solid for weeks ahead. Anyway, what would be the point of them sending one car down there when they probably have three or four a week which need to be disposed of? Another consideration is that before sending a car to auction, it will be necessary to spend time cleaning it up first and, because garages have to give priority to the cars they are retailing, it is very rare that they can spare the time or personnel to do this either. This is why the trade dealer plays such a vital role in the heirarchy of the used car business; in fact, without him, the motor trade could not operate at all, which is why you will usually enjoy a cordial, indeed even a friendly welcome at most garages you approach.

Even if your wad only extends to a couple of hundred quid, this should prove no barrier to you starting your career as a trade dealer, providing you can bluff your way just a little in the early stages. As is the case with all business, the beginning is obviously the most awkward stage because you will not be able to afford the better cars which are offered to you. Never be embarrassed to admit that you are only looking at the banger end of the market in the early stages, it may well lead to you becoming popular because often garages find these the most difficult to shift because most traders want better cars. You may also feel like this in a year or two, once you have the capital behind you, and have become choosy as well! So don't despair, someone has to shift the shrapnel after all, and as they say in the trade, 'many a banger man has become a millionaire!'.

Once you have made an acquisition, clean it up properly following the guidelines described in a later chapter, and then enter it into your local auction. As a very rough guide on pricing for the moment, any 1983-1986 banger which is basically sound with a decent length of ticket on it should be bought as a 'trade-off' for between £150 and £300. When cleaned up and placed in an auction, you should be able to clear between £100 and £300 after auctioneers' fees and expenses have been deducted. As you start to turn over more cars, your overheads will, in fact, fall because you will become eligible for trade reductions on auctioneers' fees.

The profit margins in selling cars at auction in this way may not be as broad as they would be if you were to retail the vehicles, but this is the short term sacrifice that you need to make for the benefit of building up a proper business and making a great deal more money in the medium and long term. Never forget that you are also playing safe this way, because you are buying cars in the safest way and selling them in the safest way with no comebacks, and with guaranteed payment at the end of each week for the cars you have sold in the form of an auctioneer's cheque. I cannot emphasise enough how important it is not to be tempted to fall into the trap of trying to 'rag' cars like this through the papers because this is where most people go wrong. Think in terms of embarking on a career and the importance of building a good reputation, both in the trade and then later in retailing. It is impossible to build a good reputation selling shrapnel to the public, so don't even try it. Stick with the auctions until you can afford to buy really decent motors.

THE TALE OF TWO DEALERS

To help us look at the pros and cons of the two different ways of starting up, let us follow the fortunes of two imaginary car dealers. Dealer No. 1 is our hero, Terry 'The Trader'; Dealer No. 2 is Ralph the 'Rag-It' merchant.

These two chaps know each other and, having made the decision to go into the motor trading business independently, agree to run a competition between themselves to see which one of them can make the most money within their first year of business.

Ralph is impatient to make a fast buck without giving any consideration to long term goals. Within a couple of days he picks up a banger in the local auction, cleans it up and sticks it in the local rag. Over the following weekend he sells it to a 'punter' and clears a healthy £200 which leaves him feeling well pleased with himself. In the meantime, Terry has visited a few local garages looking for trade-offs. Having finally settled on a reasonably clean motor, he too cleans it up and then sticks it in the local auction at the end of the week. It goes under the hammer and he clears, after auctioneers' fees, just over £100. Comparing notes the following week, Ralph is convinced that Terry was foolish to have thrown away potential profit by sticking the car in the auction rather than selling it through the local paper. Terry tries to persuade him that he has other objectives in mind, but to no avail.

Three months later

Three months later finds them both still going about the business in their different ways. Terry can now afford to buy a couple of trade-offs a week from the garages and is still sticking them in the local auction. He averages around £200 between the two which comes in regularly at the end of each week in the form an auctioneer's cheque. He realises that this is only a modest start but is content in the knowledge that he is laying the groundwork for a much more lucrative future by establishing and nurturing contacts within the trade.

On the face of it, Ralph is doing the better of the two. He is selling about three cars a fortnight and averages around £300 a week. He still considers Terry crazy to throw away potential profit by not retailing the cars and frequently tells him so. He thinks his business is fantastic, the only drawback he would admit to is the hassle he has to put up with from time-wasters and the cash flow difficulties associated with getting the money through from his punters in time to purchase fresh cars and keep his business running.

Six months later

Six months down the line and the situation is beginning to change. Terry has now caught up with Ralph. He is buying about three to four cars out of the trade each week and is bringing in around £350 average after expenses. Ralph is still beavering away and earns about the same, although, by now, he is just beginning to appreciate the difficulties of making a consistent living from dealing in cars his way. For instance, there was a bad patch in August when, due to the holiday season, he didn't manage to shift even one motor throughout the whole month. Luckily, he made a real killing out of an old BMW at the beginning of September with a profit of £1,400 which evened the matter out, but it was a close shave which unsettled him. It was this experience which, for the first time, caused him to envy Terry his more consistent and secure method of dealing. He is also surprised to discover that his friend has now caught up with him earningswise. Secretly he is beginning to have doubts but although he doesn't know it, 'he ain't seen nothing yet!'.

What Ralph has yet to realise is that whilst he may have made more money during this initial six-month period than his friend Terry, he can only progress from this point on very slowly. In fact, he almost reached his maximum earning potential in the first week because, even with the help of the odd extra profitable deal now and then, like the BMW, he will discover at the end of the year that he will have averaged less than he would have expected due to the odd bad patch here and there. Terry, on the other hand, may not have been making so much immediate profit up until this point, but what he has been doing will prove far more rewarding in the long term. Time spent during this period in gradually building a network of contacts and laying the foundations of a proper business will soon reap the rewards of a patiently sown harvest and to a degree which will amaze his friend Ralph.

Nine months later

At the nine-month point, the process has already begun. Terry is buying more cars per week with far less effort now. Less effort because, instead of having to hunt around garages, they are ringing him up and offering him cars. He has established a reputation for himself as a reliable chap which goes a long way in the motor trade. He has always proved punctual, courteous and easy to deal with. Being a naturally shrewd individual, he appreciated the importance of not being a niggler. Realising all cars have faults, he never tried to beat the garages down over small problems which he knew would not affect his profit margins when he put the vehicles into auction. The garages have been quick to appreciate this professional attitude, and have begun to favour him over the other traders operating in the area. He is now averaging about five cars a week and employs a part-time driver to help him get the cars to auction. Because he has more money to play with, he is in the position to pick the odd one or two slightly cleaner and newer cars in amongst the shrapnel which have helped to raise his average profit to around £150 per vehicle after expenses. Very few weeks go by in which he doesn't see a clear £700-£800, and the money is still coming in regularly in the form of an auctioneer's cheque at the end of the week. He is already beginning to consider having a dabble at some of the more expensive cars in the £2,000-£3,000 range that his friends, as they have now become, in the garages are offering him.

Ralph, on the other hand, is beginning to have doubts at last. He now openly envies Terry getting paid up regularly by the auctioneers instead of having to cope as he does with people who leave deposits and then clear off never to be seen again. Another inexplicable bad patch of two solid weeks has knocked his average down a bit and to cap it all, a punter to whom he sold a car some weeks back has kicked up a fuss about it and threatened to go to the Trading Standards Office. Normally, it would have been Ralph's policy to have bought the car back straightaway to keep the peace but now, because he has a bit of a cash flow problem, he can't afford to do this and is just hoping it will all die down.

12 months later

As the anniversary for their sortie into the motor dealing world looms, Terry has shot so far ahead of his friend that by now there is no comparison between them. His businesslike attitude has stood him in good stead and his reputation for being a fair chap to deal with has spread amongst garages in the area. He is now buying cars thick and fast, and is even in the position to be choosy. He does about four or five bangers and two newer cars a week which clears him at least £1,000 a week. He is now running a proper business.

His mate Ralph is still effectively just a backstreet car dealer who, now that he is forced to calculate his earnings properly for the year, is surprised to find that, bad patches taken into account, he has averaged far less than he was expecting. He is also thoroughly disillusioned because he has been prosecuted over the bad car which the punter complained about. He wishes dearly that he had demonstrated the same patience and foresight as Terry.

This little story demonstrates the concept of trade dealing quite well. See how Terry, within the space of just one year, has already established a business which is paying him the equivalent to an annual salary of £50,000. By the end of his second year, he will have bettered that considerably.

At first sight it seems impossible that he could have achieved this so quickly until you stop to consider what factors he had on his side. For instance, one of the key aspects of his success was the lack of overheads necessary to start and run this enterprise. The statistics show that four out of five small businesses which fail in their first year, do so through a combination of cash flow difficulties and unnecessary overheads.

WHAT DID TERRY NEED TO SUCCEED?

Right, so what did Terry need in the first place to make this new business succeed? Well firstly, he needed a continuous supply of suitable vehicles; hundreds of them continuously on tap for him to pick and choose his 'profit earners' from. If he had to fund and set up such an organisation to provide this service, it would cost a fortune. However, he doesn't have to, because it already exists in the form of dozens of local garages paying the rent and wages necessary to supply Terry with his cars. All he has to do is drive them home. Actually, in the initial stages at least, he doesn't really need premises himself because all he does is wash and clean up cars which he can either do outside his house or sub-contract to a valeting service.

That takes care of that then, so what else does he need? Well, he needs an organisation large and efficient enough to sell on his cars almost as quickly as he buys them, whilst at the same time providing a foolproof payment collection service to ensure he incurs no bad debts which would affect cash flow. Not only that, but also this organisation must ensure that he has no warranty or comeback problems in relation to the vehicles he sells, all of which cost money to solve. Again, to create such an organisation would incur enormous overheads, but he doesn't need to, since it already exists in the form of local auctions. Sure, he has to pay a small commission on each vehicle sold, but not until it has already earned its profit for him, so again he lets the local auction pay the rent and wages to collect and process his money for him. He is laughing all the way to the proverbial bank!

SYNOPSIS OF TERRY'S SUCCESS

1. No rent required for premises.

2. No staff wages.

3. Fast cash flow.

4. Guaranteed payment - no bad debts.

5. No borrowings required - thanks to rapid capital growth.

6. No warranty or comeback expenses due to auction protection.

THE LEGAL IMPLICATIONS OF TRADE BUYING

It is important, before you get too carried away and rush off to your nearest garage, that you realise some of the legal implications of becoming a trade buyer. If you go to a garage and declare yourself to be a trader, you buy a car on trade terms. This means you lose all your rights in law under the Sale of Goods Act and you may have no official comeback if something proves subsequently to be wrong with the vehicle. This is only fair; as a trader it is up to you to assess the vehicle and the risks involved in purchasing it. However, bearing in mind the aforementioned opportunities to inspect vehicles properly before buying, the problem should never really arise unless you are exceptionally unlucky. If you are doing the job properly, you ought to be making very good money out of trade buying and therefore you have to take the philosophical viewpoint that on occasion there is the very slight possibility of the odd loss. Bear in mind, however, that you would be running a much higher risk of this if you were buying these old cars 'as seen' at auction.

There is no individual more despised in the motor trade than a chap who calls himself a trader, buys a car on trade terms and then comes back screaming if something proves to be wrong. Few people who have done this get the chance to purchase on trade terms again, word spreads fast.

ESTABLISHING YOURSELF

In order to become successful as a trade dealer it is necessary to endear yourself to the garages which are going to be able to supply you with a steady flow of cars. The shrewdest way to do this is to identify which these garages are likely to be by dropping in on all the garages in your area regularly and noting how many trade-ins any particular place takes in during a week. When you have identified the garages you have to concentrate on, take a leaf out of our friend Terry's book and start to establish a reputation for yourself by being straightforward and easy to deal with. Reliability and punctuality are qualities which are admired in any line of business, but none more so than the motor trade. Carrying cash and paying on the nose, rather than with a promise, also ensures that when some tasty trade-in comes in through the door, it will be your number which the sales department ring first.

Another leaf out of Terry's book, don't be a niggler. If you are being offered a reasonable car at a reasonable price, providing it tests okay and you know that you can make a profit on it, offer a reasonable shout for it and impress them by accepting the occasional motor which has an obvious but unimportant fault which you know will not affect your profit at auction. Don't lean too heavily on minor faults in the bargaining process; err on the generous side within reason, of course. This kind of behaviour will pay you dividends in the end because you will simply be offered more cars than your rivals. Garages are not generally used to traders treating them with much respect so if you make

28

an effort to charm them a little, you shouldn't have much trouble in establishing yourself as the top man in the district.

Once you have established a working relationship with a particular garage and you know that you can trust their description of vehicles over the phone, you can consider 'underwriting' cars; in other words, guaranteeing to pay a price for them on collection. Once any garage has decided that you are their top trader, they are not going to risk losing you by selling you a dud car through inadequate description. Frankly, they would probably rather stand the loss themselves. Remember, all any garage wants to do is to shift its trade-in cars and get its money back on them as quickly as possible. Any trader who handles the whole matter in a really professional way will always impress them.

HOW TO BEAT THE COMPETITION

If you find for any reason that there is tough competition in the garages with which you are attempting to establish yourself as a trader, then the best way of getting your foot in the door is simply to offer them a bit over the odds for the vehicles. If you are not sure how to value them, go about it like this. First of all, spend a few days down at your local auction looking at specific models of cars and note the kind of prices which reasonably cleaned up examples make. Work out your average prices for these models to within £50 or so. When a similar model comes up in a garage as a trade-off, offer them £100 below that figure. You will almost certainly find that it is you who will drive the car away for the simple reason that the other traders are almost certainly offering at least £50 less again. As long as you know you that are going to make a small profit to start with, you can't really go wrong.

CHAPTER THREE

TRADE DEALING THROUGH AUCTIONS

There is another way of trade dealing which is to buy and sell cars just within the auction system, i.e. you buy from an auction in one area of the country and sell in another. The motor trade, like most traditional occupations, is riddled with mythology and folklore. If you hang around motor traders for more than ten minutes, you will start hearing tales of how cars are always sold in auctions much cheaper 'up the line'. Wherever you are in the country, according to motor dealing folklore, there is always a mythical auction further north at which cars are sold cheaper! In my own experience, this has not proved true. Having invested considerable time and expense travelling to every major auction in the country, as far as I have ever been able to tell, there is no significant price difference between any of them when the relative *condition* of the vehicles is taken into account. Motor dealing folklore does not take into account that vehicles deteriorate much quicker in some parts of the country than in others due to climatic differences and in particular the quantity of road salt used during the winter months. As a general rule, cars in the north are in worse condition for their age than their counterparts in the south. In most cases, when the true cost of putting these northern cars into a similar condition to their counterparts in the south is taken into consideration, it will prove cheaper for the prudent buyer to pay a little more in a southern auction in the first place.

Largely due to this well-established folklore, the motor trade generally is obsessed with the idea of bringing cars from the north to the south. Now here is an interesting observation. I have always noticed when attending northern auctions that on the rare occasion when a particularly clean car comes under the hammer, it always makes an exceptionally high price for its age. If I were to experiment with shifting cars between auctions now, I would seriously look into the idea of transporting good clean cars from the south up to the north! Because my motor dealing career led me off in other directions, I never had time to play around with this concept, so I can't promise it would work, but it might be worth a try. You never know, you might even make your fortune from this alone!

What I think actually lies behind this 'up the line' myth, as I refer to it, is this. In motor trading, like most other businesses, you only tend to hear about the exceptional profits rather than the everyday deals. Every trader has his favourite auction story. But, what you have to ask yourself is this, if this chap really believed he could get deals like this every time at that particular auction, firstly, why on earth would he tell anyone else about it? And secondly, why isn't he up there every week buying cars? The obvious answer is because he knows only too well that it was an exceptional incident. It stands to reason in terms of mathematical probability that if you spend your whole life at car auctions buying and selling cars, you are bound to pick up the odd exceptional bargain.

I certainly hope that I have not discouraged you from attempting to buy and sell cars between auctions if you want to, because there is no doubt that some people do it quite successfully. However, what I would say is this. Firstly, it is very unlikely that you will be able to make a success of doing this with the shrapnel if you have to travel considerable distances between sales. Profit margins are almost certainly going to be too narrow to justify the expenditure that you will incur shifting the cars about. Secondly, if you are going to do it with more expensive cars, just make absolutely certain that you are sure of your prices before you commit too much money to the project.

Whether you are buying or selling at auction, it is essential that you have an understanding of certain aspects of the auction scene. For instance, to be aware of the devious and dirty tricks that can be done to cars entered for sale 'as seen' by the unscrupulous, also how the bidding system works and how to successfully outbid the opposition. Few people realise that there is a secret language which passes between the auctioneer and the trade when a car is going under the hammer and knowledge of this is very useful too. I have covered all this in a later chapter.

You will have gathered by now, I am sure, that I have tried to discourage you for various reasons from selling direct to the public in the early stages if you can only spare the cash to deal in older cars. However, in case later on when you are buying more expensive and better quality 'trade-off' cars, you are tempted to do the odd retail sale of a good roadworthy car, or indeed, move into the retail sector by leasing or buying your own pitch, then you will find the later sections on how to advertise and how to sell a car useful.

Whichever way you decide to go about becoming a trade dealer you will be able to move up the car price hierarchy as your capital grows and soon the trade-off cars which you will be buying will bring in higher profit returns on the difference between trade and auction prices, even if the return relative to capital outlay is less. Obviously, when you are dealing with bangers, a profit margin of £100 on a £300 car is nearly 30%, whereas when you are buying a £3,000 car a profit margin of £300 will only be 10% but of course you are making a much larger profit on each car and with much less hassle because the newer cars will be more reliable and so forth.

TRADE BROKING

When you reach that happy stage of being able to buy more of the higher priced trade-offs, you may well consider doing a bit of trading between garages. Once you have established a network of contacts, you will often know where you can place a car somewhere else in the trade for a quick, modest profit. Some dealers actually set themselves up as 'trade only' wholesalers of cars; these people are referred to as 'trade brokers'. This is something you may consider doing yourself at some stage. It can prove highly lucrative. In many instances it is not necessary to hold a lot of vehicles in stock yourself. Once you have built up a network of contacts within the trade and are well known, you will be able to take a vehicle on a sale or return basis from one garage and offer it to another, taking a nice 'tickle' out of it for doing so without necessarily having to lay out any money yourself on the car at all.

Possibly even by this stage you may only wish to concentrate on the superior and better quality trade-off cars exclusively and forget about the shrapnel altogether. I suppose it depends on what is available in your area and what your individual preference is, but by this time you will probably be tired of cleaning up cars yourself and will either be sub-contracting this to a reasonably priced local valeting service, or employing a part-time pre-school leaver or perhaps a retired neighbour to do the job for you. Your time will be needed more valuably elsewhere, i.e. contacting garages, going to look at cars and shifting them between auction sites and around the trade generally. This is when you will have reached your 'banking stage' i.e. you put money out, and more money comes back in. Before you even realise it has happened, you will then wake up one day and discover that you have become a busy and successful businessman, or to put it another way, a serious career motor trader!

A 'carbuncle' taking his 'smoker' for a run to the bank!

CHAPTER FOUR

What To Look For
And What To Avoid

There are so many hundreds of different makes and models of vehicles that it is obviously impossible for me to tell you exactly which you should deal in as you progress throughout your motor trading career. As every year progresses the motor manufacturers add more and more models and model variations to their ranges. It is all quite bewildering, and one has to wonder where it is all going to end. In a few years' time the trade Price Guides are going to be as thick as *War and Peace*. Looking back even to the time when I first started motor trading in the early eighties, it seems as if there were only half as many model variations on the market then as there are today. Man has made life complicated enough as it is by inventing the motorcar without making thousands of different variations of the same theme! I reckon some of these manufacturers employ whole departments just to think up bloody silly names to stick on their cars!

Because these car ranges are now so infinite, I am not even going to attempt to draw up comprehensive lists or anything of that nature, because otherwise this book would simply end up looking like a price guide. However, I will, of course, mention the odd make and model of car by way of example or comparison. Mainly I shall attempt to discuss the principles which are involved in picking profit-earning cars so that, hopefully, you can apply these to whatever vehicles you encounter when looking around for stock.

There are a number of important criteria to which you need to give careful consideration when looking for cars to buy:

1. Popularity.
2. Insurance group.
3. Performance to economy ratio.
4. Mileage and condition.
5. Length of MOT and roadworthiness.

I have listed the above in descending order. This is based on logic, because, whilst the roadworthiness and condition of the vehicle are the most important aspects in reality, there is no point in considering these aspects on a particular vehicle unless it meets with your other qualifying criteria because you are not going to buy it anyway! Now let us look at each of these aspects a little more closely.

POPULARITY

The most obvious one really, there is no point in sticking your money into cars which you know are not popular. To this end, it is always a good thing to familiarise yourself with the best selling used cars on a national basis, and also, in particular, within your own area. One of the most surprising aspects of motor trading is that there are significant differences in the popularity of particular types of vehicles between specific areas of the country. Make a point of checking your local *AutoTrader* regularly and noting which models turn over quickest in the trade adverts. Keep an eye on local forecourts as well.

INSURANCE GROUP

As I am quite sure you are aware, the last couple of years have seen a major shake up in the insurance industry which has resulted in many models suddenly shooting up through the ratings and incurring massive increases in premiums. Interestingly enough, most insurance companies will tell you that this is due more to the increase in theft potential than a performance based bias. The hot hatches have obviously suffered the most, not so much because of their outright performance as the fact that the joyriders would rather nick a quick ride than a slow one. Always therefore be very careful to check out the current insurance status of every car that you buy. However, bear in mind that this knife is a two-edged one because these group changes can also work in your favour as well. If you happen to specialise in hot hatches because you have a ready market for them, then you can certainly pick them up a lot cheaper now than ever before!

PERFORMANCE TO ECONOMY RATIO

A vital aspect of the purchase decision making process in any punter's mind lies in his perception of what is referred to as 'performance to economy ratio'. In plain English, this is the balance of performance delivered by a vehicle, relative to its fuel consumption. Today, with the benefit of computer chip regulated engines and advanced wind tunnel developed aerodynamics, even many of the most powerful cars can deliver economy figures which a decade ago would have been unthinkable. On the flip side of the same coin, many small engined cars can also deliver a surprisingly good performance whilst running on a whiff of the proverbial oil rag. However, always be aware of the fact that many of the older models were not so well sorted in this particular area, and that some therefore have appalling P/E ratios. These are not always the large engined models either, sometimes it would appear that manufacturers have made appalling choices in engine size and power relative to body weight which has resulted in equally poor P/E ratios.

A good car dealer is always aware of the P/E lemons which almost invariably exist in virtually every manufacturer's range. Often manufacturers have created the odd inappropriate blend of engine size to body weight in order to satisfy either various marketing pressures or other criteria, such as tax breaks or price breaks. Your only defence is to know your cars well!

MILEAGE AND CONDITION

While mileage and condition often go hand in hand, this is not always the case. Sometimes that 'one lady owner, low mileage

Cavalier', which has actually suffered four years of transporting dogs to school and young children to animal training classes, is in much worse nick than a high mileage rep-driven version of the same model which has carried only a driver and perhaps a few lightweight samples in the boot for all of its operational life! Any oil company will tell you that it is a scientifically proven fact that an engine which has only been used for short journeys around town will have worn far more significantly than an identical engine which has been run at a constant operating temperature for a much higher mileage over the same time period. This also applies to gearboxes, axles and most other mechanical components too.

Unfortunately, we live in a society which bases a great deal of emphasis on mileage in relation to the value of vehicles, so assessing any particular vehicle which has a high mileage but is in good condition, is always a difficult juggling act. Bear in mind that due to the recent increase in popularity of diesel cars, attitudes are at least changing in relation to them. Common sense dictates this is a nonsense, of course, because whilst it may be true that diesel engines themselves can take higher mileages than their petrol-fuelled counterparts, gearboxes, axles and all other components will wear at exactly the same rate, a fact which does not seem to have been taken into consideration at all! But then again, a lot of factors which go into car valuation are complete nonsense!

LENGTH OF MOT AND ROADWORTHINESS

We will be covering both these topics comprehensively elsewhere, but they cannot be emphasised enough, so here we go! Firstly, it is never safe to buy a car with a short MOT unless you are a hundred per cent confident that you know exactly how much it will cost you to renew it and allow this in your bid price. Secondly, it is never safe to sell an unroadworthy car at all!

BE CLEAR ABOUT YOUR PRIORITIES

The first thing to do when you start to search for suitable vehicles, whether in trade or at auction, is to be certain that you are clear in your mind about precisely what you are doing. You are out to make money out of them, not to buy them for your own personal use and, that being so, you must empty your head of all preconceived notions and prejudices concerning cars that you may have held previously. Keep in mind that you are looking for a car which you can shift as quickly as possible with a decent profit margin, so your purchasing criteria may now be entirely different to any which you have employed in the past when looking for your own cars. This means you may well have to seek out cars that you personally dislike. What you have to realise is that if you go after the right sort of cars, it is unlikely that you will get stuck with them provided you buy them at the right price and you have prepared them properly for sale. However, if you go and buy the wrong sort of cars, you are on to a loser before you start. Remember, in the early stages, you may not have enough money to spare to tide you over if you make the wrong decision.

First golden rule

The first golden rule, particularly in the early stages when you don't have enough money to afford a mistake, is never to buy a car with a short MOT. If possible, never buy one with less than six months' MOT unless it possesses such good qualities otherwise that you feel that you can risk dropping below this 'plimsoll line' by a month or so. Once you have become established as a trade buyer and are well known at your local garages, they will usually oblige you by putting a roadworthy car through a new MOT if you are prepared to pay a little more for it. This is always worthwhile if the car has a short ticket. This rule is particularly important when buying at auction. No matter how good a car looks at a sale, unless it is incredibly cheap and you are confident that you can replace everything on it which it may require to bring it up to MOT standard, leave it alone. Always assume that a nice looking car at an auction with a short MOT means that the people who have entered the motor know that it is going to cost a fortune to get a new ticket!

Second golden rule

The second golden rule is that it is always worth paying a little more than the going rate for a vehicle which is basically clean rather than ultra cheap and tatty. What I mean by 'basically clean' is a car which when cleaned up will look like a nice respectable motor that has always been well cared for. This sort of vehicle will always sell fast. Most vehicles actually sell on first impressions, or, to put it another way, 'love at first sight'.

Third golden rule

The third golden rule, which applies to the early stages when you have to play ultra safe, is to avoid buying foreign cars if possible. Surprisingly, there is still a substantial degree of bigotry in the used car market concerning foreign models, particularly the further down the price range and into the shrapnel territory that you go. There is a certain logic behind this; people fear the cost of foreign replacement parts and generally believe that foreign cars cost more to put right. Whilst neither of these beliefs necessarily hold true in every case, it is, nevertheless, worth recognising that this is a consideration in the used car market. Back when I first started, the bigotry was very deeply rooted indeed. Since then it has relaxed somewhat but is nevertheless still there. Over a period of years, this situation will probably change. It is important to realise that makes like Ford, many of whose models are actually made abroad in places like Germany, are still considered to be British by the average used car punter simply because the parts and labour involved in repairing them have always been on a par with BL/Austin/Rover models.

SYNOPSIS OF WHAT TO LOOK FOR

1. Start with a narrow field of bread-and-butter cars, avoid being adventurous or you might get stuck with a landmark!

2. Never buy a car with a short MOT unless you are absolutely convinced that you know how much it will cost you to get a new one for it.

3. Better to pay a bit more for a basically clean car than to go for a cheaper, tatty one.

4. In the early stages, try to avoid buying foreign cars.

EXAMPLES OF CARS TO GO LOOKING FOR
WHEN STARTING OUT

Models mentioned mean all versions/engine sizes unless otherwise mentioned. Cars are in alphabetical not priority order.

Alfa Romeo	New 33 (90 on), 75
Audi	80, 90, Coupe 1.8, Coupe GT 2.0, 100, Avant 1.8, Avant 2.0, Avant 2.2
Austin	Mini (1988 on), Metro 1.3 (1988 on) except MG Turbo
BMW	316, 318i, 320i, 323i, 325i, 518, 520i, 525i, 328i
Citroen	2CV, AX, BX
Fiat	Panda, 4x4 (1990 on), new Uno, Tipo 1.7 Diesel, Tempra 1.9 Diesel
Ford	Escort, Sierra, Fiesta, Orion
Honda	Civic, Accord, Aerodeck, Prelude
Mazda	323
Peugeot	205, 309, 405
Renault	New 5 (1988 on), 9, 11, 19, 21
Rover	Metro, 213, 214, 216, 218, 414, 416, 418, 820, 825 Diesel
Saab	99, 90, 900 (except Turbo), 900i, 9000i, 9000i 2.3
Suzuki	SJ410, SJ413
Vauxhall	Nova, Astra, Belmont, Cavalier, Calibra, Carlton
Volkswagen	Polo, Golf, Scirocco, Passat
Volvo	340 (1988 on), 440, 460, 240

This list is not meant in any way, shape or form to be comprehensive or exclusive of other models. It is intended purely as a guide to the *sort* of vehicles you should be looking for.

Avoid being adventurous
or you might get stuck with a landmark!
– p. 40

CHAPTER FIVE

WHAT TO LOOK FOR
WHEN INSPECTING A CAR

BODYWORK AND GENERAL VISIBLE CONDITION

The importance of the general appearance of the vehicle cannot be emphasised enough in relation to motor trading. Basically, the cleaner a car is, the quicker it will sell, and if you are retailing to the public, the less hassle and comeback you will get. People are prepared to forgive the odd little problems that any used car inevitably has if the overall appearance is smart and tidy.

The first thing to do when assessing a car is to walk around it and look for any signs of serious accident damage, i.e. do the doors and panels line up properly? Indeed, are there any gaps between the panels? If there is any light damage, such as scratches or minor parking dents or even light surface corrosion bubbling through paint, assess whether it is a colour that you will be able to match up successfully, either with an aerosol spray yourself or economically at a bodyshop. Unfortunately, as the finishes on cars vary so much today, knowledge on this point only comes with experience. The obvious golden rule here is that if the paint is metallic, you will not be able to match it yourself and, whether metallic or not, avoid cars which need paint in the middle of panel sections, i.e. dents in the middle of a door, bonnet or boot panel, because any repair spray job here that you may do yourself will show. However, if all that is needed is some touch-up work on the edge of a panel, like the bottom of a door or the lip of a wheel arch, then you should be able to do a reasonable job providing the colour isn't too hard to match and assuming, of course, that it is not metallic.

As you walk around the car try to spot any areas which have been repaired with body filler or fibreglass. If the job has been botched the contour of the bodywork may look wrong in the area of the repair and close inspection may reveal evidence of rubbing down marks under the paint or even tiny holes in the filler. Not a bad idea to carry a powerful little magnet wrapped in a thin bit of cloth (so that it won't mark the paintwork) and try it on obvious paint repairs to see how much, if any, 'pudding' is under them.

Next, open all doors and run your fingers lightly along the inside bottom edges of them (be very careful; if there is bad rust you can get a nasty cut!). These door bottoms should be relatively rust free, certainly there should not be any bad holes.

Next, open the bonnet. If the catch is broken, grab a handful of the outer cable under the dashboard and pull it. This normally does the trick. Take a long look under the bonnet to see if everything is in its correct place and whilst you are there, do the mechanical checks which I shall describe in a minute. Look for signs of body rot and welding, particularly around the bottom chassis rail and in the area where the front shock absorbers and/or MacPhearson struts are mounted. Also, look for crumpled metal along the chassis and in the wings either side of the engine which would indicate accident damage.

Next, walk around to the boot and take a long look inside. Particularly if you are buying shrapnel at auction, it is essential to check the insides of boots before bidding. The interior of a boot can hide a multitude of sins, not least of which can be rotting metal around the rear suspension mounts. I cannot emphasise enough that buying a car without looking in the boot is like playing Russian roulette. Always be very suspicious of a car if for some reason or another someone has tried to stop you from looking in the boot. In fact, my advice is not to buy it. The same applies to a mysteriously locked engine compartment. Particularly at auction, always be suspicious of a car that is being kept locked in the car park until the driver comes to drive it through the ring. There is usually a good reason for this, such as the owner not wanting anyone to see inside the bonnet and discover accident damage, bodged welding or the fact that the '1600 Cavalier' is really a 1400 with a 1600 badge on it, for instance.

So, having looked over the top bodywork, doors, bonnet and boot, if you are still interested, kneel down on your old price guide or whatever, and peer underneath. Do this about three-quarters of the way along the car towards the rear so that you can check the rear suspension mounts for bad rust. If there is any, leave the car; it is unroadworthy and won't pass its next MOT without extensive work. Check also for obvious holes under the front and rear floor pans and see how much the exhaust has been bodged and then look at the sills. Actually, sills are relatively cheap so, in themselves, providing that there is sound bodywork behind them, this need not be the end of the world. Before you get up, look at the tyre tread giving special attention to inner edges and signs of uneven wear indicating bad tracking or crash damage. Remember, any bald patch on a tyre makes it illegal for you to sell the car with that tyre on. Calculate any replacement cost in your bids for the vehicle.

If you are buying at auction it is not a bad idea to have a notebook with you in order to make a few short notes about any particular vehicle along with its lot number. When it comes into the ring, this makes it much easier to protect yourself from becoming too carried away. I say this in the light of bitter experience, because at one time or another all of us in the trade have forgotten about some serious fault with a car on display in the auction car park and then have paid too much for it! Usually remembering all the terrible things that were wrong with the darn thing about two seconds after the hammer has gone down! Seriously, this is a very important tip, and I would suggest that you jot down notes something along the following lines:

Lot 69 Escort 1400, needs - 2 tyres - rear exhaust box - indicator lens.

Having looked under both sides, take a quick dive under the front. Look for crash damage to the front suspension or clues like bits of grass and mud stuck anywhere indicating a recent off-road excursion! Check for leaking brake hoses, disc callipers/drums and leaking shock absorbers. Then do the same at the rear, checking for leaking shock absorbers, petrol leaks from the tank and leaking brake hoses and drums/disc calipers again. Also rusty spring hangers and rear exhaust box condition. If all this is satisfactory, start on the mechanical tests.

This all sounds terribly time consuming, but remember, you are not doing it to every car in the garage in the case of buying 'trade-offs', or in the case of auctions, you are only doing it to those cars in the car park which you are interested in. This means that out of perhaps one hundred cars, you will be only seriously inspecting a dozen or so. Also, having done this quick checkover once or twice, you will find yourself rattling it off in a matter of a couple of minutes or so.

The only thing that I haven't mentioned yet is interior. This is, obviously, common sense. Don't worry too much about the condition of carpets, particularly the front ones which are usually the most worn, because you can always get cheap replacements from scrap yards, or even a couple of new floor mats which will do wonders for the appearance of the car. Front seats likewise are easily covered.

CHECK LIST:

1. General appearance

Bodywork/interior

Boot and bonnet

Doors

2. Underneath each side

Rear suspension

Floor pans

Sills

Exhaust

Tyres

3. *Underneath front and back*

Front suspension

Rear suspension mounts

Petrol tank

Exhaust

Shock absorber leaks

Brake fluid leaks on drums - disc calipers/hoses

CLOCKED CARS

The quickest give away to a clocked car is its interior. When people clock cars, they usually make the mistake of over-doing it, i.e. they wind an 85,000-miler back to 35,000 instead of leaving it at something believable like 55,000. Consequently, you can nearly always spot when a motor has had a 'haircut' by the general wear and tear of the seats and carpets, and the brake, clutch and accelerator pedals.

Once you think you have smelt out a 'cuckoo', take a closer look at the crosshead screws which hold the instrument panel on. Very few people bother to use the right size of screwdriver so they usually leave tell-tale slip marks and burrs on the screws. People don't clock speedos by winding them back with electric drills and all that nonsense you hear from people who don't know what they are talking about. What 'clockers' actually do is pull the instrument panel off and move the first figure around against its ratchet. If they don't do this properly, when the mileometer starts moving again the first digits slip out of line, which is a dead giveaway.

Everyone has their cuckoo stories, so here's mine. I pulled the instrument panel out on a car once to replace a blown bulb in a speedo and I found a jam label on the back of it which read *'Oh no, not again!'*.

CHAPTER SIX

MECHANICAL TESTS

Would it surprise you if I told you that most motor dealers have a relatively limited mechanical knowledge? Certainly most of them develop an ability over the years to spot problems but very few of the people who really make the most money out of cars actually get their hands dirty fixing them.

It is important to realise that it is quite possible for someone to train themselves to identify faults in motor vehicles without necessarily having the practical ability to put those problems right. For instance, by knowing what to listen for it is possible to spot the difference between drive-shaft whine and worn wheel bearings, or whether that hideous noise in the engine is due to worn camshaft bearings or big ends. Whether or not you know how to fix these things is irrelevant. What is most important is that you diagnose it correctly because then experience will remind you how much it will cost to put this right, which, of course, is vital when buying vehicles.

Obviously, as cars are made up of thousands of mechanical components, it is not possible to cover every aspect and every potential problem here. If you do not possess much mechanical ability yourself, then again it is all the more important, particularly in the early stages, that you stick with a narrow range of basically simple, reliable cars. This way you will quickly become conversant with each model and learn to identify a bad example, even if you don't know what its exact problem is. Furthermore, should you get stuck with a bit of a 'lemon', because there will be an abundance of cheap second-hand parts, it shouldn't cost you a fortune to put the matter right. This is another good reason for staying away from foreign cars at the cheaper end of the market.

ENGINES

When inspecting a car, there are certain specific tests which you should do to safeguard yourself from buying a lemon. First of all, before you start the engine, open the bonnet and, having made sure that the radiator is cool enough, take off the cap and look at the water *(never remove the cap on a hot radiator or you are likely to get some nasty scalds!).* If there isn't any water, leave the car alone but assuming that there is some, look for traces of oil in it. If you are unsure about this, stick your finger in the water and, having pulled it out, rub it against your thumb. If it feels slimy and slightly gritty at the same time, there may be oil in the water which could mean the head gasket is on the point of blowing or has already done so. If there is any sign of horrible frothy white muck on the cap or in the filling neck, it probably already has done! Secondly, check the dipstick and look for bubbles in the oil. There are usually one or two but if there is an abundance of bubbles on the dipstick, this can also be an indication of the same problem, i.e. water in the oil.

Now listen to the engine when it starts. If it starts with a horrible rattle even if the noise disappears straightaway, walk away from the car; either the big or small ends may be on the way out. If it starts smoothly, see whether it revs smoothly without making an undue noise. In many cars, for instance, the overhead camshafts rattle if the bearings are worn in the head. The time to pay most attention to an engine is when it slows down; listen for rattles or rumbles. Rattles can indicate big end wear on the crank, rumbles can indicate main bearing wear. If you are unsure about noises, develop a habit of listening to some of your neighbours' or friends' cars which you know have good engines, so that you will recognise a bad one in a similar model when you come across it.

Always be suspicious of an engine which isn't willing to rev freely and starts to stutter at high revs. An old trick to disguise big end rattles at tickover is to deliberately retard the ignition timing. The unscrupulous can get away with this sort of dirty trick at auctions sometimes, where car engines are not normally revved very high.

Another useful test that can be done while the engine is running is to pull off the oil filler cap *(always watch out for the rotating fan, **never** do this test with loose shirt sleeves or clothing)* and look to see if oil is blowing out under pressure when you grab the throttle cable and blip the engine. If there was not much oil on the dipstick when you checked it, place your hand over the oil filler orifice and feel for pressure. If there is more than a gentle flutter on your fingers, it means the piston rings are worn. Bear in mind, though, that this has to be serious to prevent you from buying a car which is otherwise smart and has a decent length of ticket on it, because after all, if it is an old car, it is bound to pass some oil. Providing it goes all right, that is all that really matters. However, by doing these tests on every car you inspect, you will learn to spot extreme cases when they crop up and therefore be in a position to decide whether or not to go for a certain vehicle.

Always worth remembering, if you have a chance to get a car's engine warm before buying, do so, because this is when the majority of problems will show up. When an engine is cold, for instance, the oil is thicker and this can often disguise serious bearing wear for a surprisingly long time until the engine has become hot enough for the oil to thin out, which is when the noise starts and you realise something is wrong. Again, at auctions, be aware of the fact that the unscrupulous can prolong this process via the use of ultra thick oil additives. These additives are all right when used correctly, but unfortunately, unscrupulous people occasionally abuse their intended use by adding four or five cans to a sump. This can disguise bearing wear and prevent the low oil pressure warning light coming on at tickover. When buying cars 'as seen' at auction, you are at your most vulnerable to this nasty trick. There is no real safeguard except to say, if possible, pay more attention to any car with a cold engine (perhaps deliberately driven in as early as possible to allow the engine maximum time to cool before sale) than one at normal temperature. The easiest way of assessing engine temperature is to feel the outside top of the radiator *(once again, watch out for the fan if you are doing this with the engine at tickover)*. If the radiator feels really warm then the engine should be hot enough to show up any problems. However, if the radiator feels cool to the touch, these problems may not show up. It is as simple as that. You can sometimes spot when an engine has had a lot of ultra thick oil dumped into it when it starts from cold. The thick oil causes such a drag that sometimes the engine will only turn over very slowly and be reluctant to start.

Obviously when running a car's engine, there shouldn't be a lot of oily black or blue smoke emitting from the exhaust, nor, indeed, clouds of white smoke except when it is running on choke, of course. The way to test for a badly worn engine is to rev it up, hold it at reasonably high revs for a few seconds, then let the revs die gradually. When it is back on tickover, blip the accelerator again. If it then blows out a great blob of black or blue smoke, you know the piston rings are worn. If the car is still emitting clouds of white smoke after the engine has been warmed up and the choke is off, then suspect a blowing head gasket.

If the car that you are inspecting is normally fitted with an oil pressure gauge, familiarise yourself with the normal pressure readings, always taking into account the temperature of the engine at the time, i.e. a cold engine will always show a higher oil pressure at tickover than a hot one. Still on the subject of oil pressure, always look for the oil light before starting the engine. For instance, when you turn the ignition key, is it showing at all? It is not unknown for the lead to the oil warning light to 'fall off' (funny how often it seems to happen to auction cars, isn't it?). Assuming that the oil light is working, it should show before the engine starts and then go out within a couple of seconds of it running. When the engine is warm and idling, the light should never come on. However, don't mistake it for the alternator light as this frequently comes on, particularly in older cars at slow tickover.

CLUTCH

When you do have a chance to test out a car, there is a handy test for finding out how good or bad the clutch is. However, this test should only be done in a safe situation *(don't do it with anybody or anything in front of the car!)*. Firstly, sit in the driver's seat with the engine running, and, pressing the clutch pedal to the floor, engage first gear. Resting the heel of your right foot on the footbrake, pull the handbrake on hard and with the toes of the right foot, rev the car up to about half engine speed and hold it there. Then let the clutch out slowly whilst still keeping the brakes on; if the revs die or the car stalls, the clutch is okay but if it keeps revving, the clutch is slipping. Actually, a bad clutch is not the end of the world in an otherwise good car. Today these 'While You Wait' clutch and brake places can whip a new one into the average car at a fairly reasonable price. If you are concentrating on a fairly narrow range of vehicles, it is a very good idea to familiarise yourself with the general replacement costs of items like clutches and brakes.

GEARBOXES AND AXLES

When test driving a car, always listen for axle or drive shaft noises. Noise from the centre of the axle on a rear-wheel drive car can usually be attributed to a worn differential which is considerably more expensive to replace than wheel-bearings which, when worn, create noise at the *ends* of the axle. Actually, you can usually feel 'backlash' in a bad differential when backing off the accelerator on a test drive, but sometimes this is propshaft universal joint wear as well. However, if someone tries to tell you that a noisy rear axle just needs some oil, forget it; if it has got to the stage of being noisy, it is knackered.

In this day and age with so many vehicles being front wheel drive, it is absolutely essential to train yourself to recognise drive shaft noise attributed to worn constant-velocity joints. It is difficult to explain on paper how to identify the difference between this and really knackered front wheel-bearings, so my best advice is to find a mate with a high mileage front-wheel drive car which has knackered constant-velocity joints and familiarise yourself with the hideous sound. One test you can try is to corner the car slowly on full lock listening for clicking noises which are an indication of worn C.V. joints. When listening for worn wheel-bearings, always bear in mind that sound moves around a car in strange ways. It is not uncommon for the noise from a worn front wheel-bearing to appear to come from the diagonally opposite rear wheel!

When driving a vehicle, always test all gears including reverse. Whilst many models enjoy long gearbox life, others eat gearboxes for breakfast. Always remember, however, that reconditioned gearboxes are expensive, so bear this in mind when looking at cars.

BRAKES

Before test driving any vehicle, it is a very good idea to get into the habit of doing a simple test to check braking system pressure. *Now please pay special attention to the following because it is very important that you understand all the aspects involved; brakes are one thing you don't take chances with!*

Brake test with engine off

Because virtually all vehicles have servo-assisted brake systems these days, it is necessary to check brake pressure both *before* starting the engine and also *after* you have started it. Firstly then, when you get in the car with the engine switched off, simply press the brake pedal to the floor as hard as it will go (in one movement, *don't pump it*) and then hold the pedal there; if everything is all right, the pedal should stay firm but if there is a leak somewhere in the system, the pedal may start to go soft under your foot and creep further towards the floor. If this is the case, locate the leak as the brakes will be dangerous.

Brake test with engine on

Having satisfied yourself on the engine off brake test, *then* do this: take your foot right away from the pedal, start the engine and, having got it to tick over, do the same test again with the engine running. A point to remember here is that you must not start the engine with your foot still on the brake pedal otherwise you will get a false impression because, when you start it, the pedal may dip anyway.

When you are test driving a car, see that it pulls up smoothly and in a straight line on braking without pulling either to one side or to the other and without any squealing or graunching noises. *Naturally, take care when you are doing brake tests like this; choose a quiet spot, not a busy main road!*

ABS Test

If you are roadtesting a car with ABS fitted, you need to be sure it is working correctly, so, *having checked that the road is clear and safe,* stamp hard on the brakes and check whether the ABS light on the dashboard comes on. Be wary if it doesn't as ABS problems can prove very expensive to fix. Also, you should normally be able to feel the brakes 'pulsing' as the ABS cuts in.

SERVO TEST

This is not to be confused with the brake pressure tests that have just been described. This test is to check the efficiency of the actual *servo* unit itself. Make sure the engine is turned *off* and the handbrake is fully released. Then pump the brake pedal to ensure the vacuum reserve in the servo is completely used up. Press the pedal down quite hard and *then* start the engine. The pedal should fall once the engine starts and the servo comes into effect. If there is no movement or difference in the feel of the pedal when you start the engine, this is a fair indication that the servo isn't working properly. *Now please, once again, make absolutely certain that you understand the difference between the brake pressure tests and the brake servo test; these are very different things and the tests for them are completely the opposite of each other.*

SHOCK ABSORBERS

When you are doing the first visual inspection of the car's bodywork and general condition, check for the efficiency of the shock absorbers at each corner. Do this by pressing firmly with both hands on the car's wing and then releasing quickly, watching for the reaction. The wing should return smoothly to its original position without an excessive rocking movement; the crude rule of thumb here is that if it bounces more than one-and-a-half times, the shock is stuffed but you cannot rely on this old adage entirely because the operation of shock absorbers varies from model to model these days. However, it is easy to familiarise yourself with the characteristics of a particular model as this is a test you can do anywhere. Try the test out on a friend's car which has had its shock absorbers replaced recently or try it on a range of newish or very low mileage cars on a forecourt. Once you know what a good shock absorber feels like, you will soon learn to spot a duff one.

It is essential to master this test because to sell a car with bad shock absorbers, even one bad shock absorber, is very dangerous and illegal. Besides which, providing you allow for them in your bid price, they are not expensive to replace on run-of-the-mill stuff. Remember, however, they *cannot* just be replaced one at a time; they must be replaced in *pairs*. If there is one defective shock at the front, then **both front shock absorbers must be replaced** and the same goes for the rear of the car. Otherwise the handling of the vehicle may be upset. Frankly, it has always been my policy to replace all four shock absorbers simultaneously just to be on the safe side, but then I like to sleep nights!

STEERING

To check for wear in the steering mechanism, stand outside the car with the driver's door open or the window down and with your left hand, wobble the steering wheel from side to side whilst watching the right hand front wheel. There should be virtually no play - the wheels should react precisely to the steering wheel. If it feels loose or sloppy or indeed if you can feel or hear a definite clunk as play is taken up before the wheels begin to react to the movement of the steering wheel, it could mean that the vehicle needs a new universal joint or joints in the steering column, or perhaps new ball joints at either end of the steering rack, or even a completely new steering rack or steering box. Be very wary of steering problems unless you are knowledgeable on the subject. If you are even slightly unhappy, leave the car well alone. This is one area in which you can really dip out badly. Take no chances!

FRONT SUSPENSION

Wear in front suspension linkage is not always easy to detect and no test should be regarded as foolproof. In ideal circumstances, you should jack up the front of one side of the car so the wheel you are testing is clear of the ground, then squatting in front of it *(without putting your legs underneath the car, of course!)* grab the wheel top and bottom and shake it vigorously. If the king pin bearings are badly worn they will usually clunk when you do this. Better still, if you can take the pressure of the front spring off the bottom link by placing another jack under the spring pan and taking up the strain until the link is free, this will give you an even better idea.

In most cases you will not get the chance to jack up the front of the car, so, better than nothing, just squat in front of the wheel and, gripping it with both hands about three quarters of the way up on each side (i.e. at ten minutes to two o'clock), give it a good shake. This simple test will sometimes cause a badly worn suspension link to clunk and make itself known to you. Also, this can sometimes show up badly worn wheel-bearings.

CHAPTER SEVEN

COMPARISON OF WAYS TO OBTAIN
VEHICLES FOR STOCK

Irrespective of whether you intend to become a trade dealer or
go into retailing cars, it is useful to give objective consideration
to the pros and cons of the various methods of obtaining vehicles
for stock. One method may be more suited to a particular form
of motor trading than another.

BUYING FROM NEWSPAPERS
Pros
1. You know what you are buying because you get a chance to
   inspect it properly.

2. You can often make an assessment of how it has been driven
   and treated because you can meet the owner.

Cons
1. Very time consuming way of obtaining stock because it can
   involve a good deal of travelling between individual vehicles,
   many of which you will not buy for one reason or another.

2. Difficult to obtain vehicles below market value this way
   because you will be in competition with the general public for
   popular and saleable cars. Owners may not feel it necessary to
   accept 'trade price' offers.

3. When buying more expensive cars this way, you run a
   considerable risk of buying vehicles which are still in the legal
   possession of HP companies or on lease agreement. This is

why most motor dealers subscribe to an organisation like *HP Information PLC* (see 'How To Get Trade Benefits' section).

BUYING AT AUCTION

Pros

1. Wide choice of vehicles in one location, cuts down all running around time.

2. Normally, you have automatic protection from losing your money should you buy a vehicle at auction which is stolen, still on HP or turns out to be an insurance write-off, because you are protected by the auction's Indemnity Scheme. (However, always check the details of the Indemnity Scheme run by any particular auction before bidding.)

3. Swift and efficient; you buy cars with cash and drive them away there and then.

4. Normally, when buying warranted vehicles sold 'as good', you have until one hour after the sale ends to reject them which gives you time to take them to a local garage and have them inspected. (Again, check the details of the buying 'as good' policy at any particular auction before bidding.)

Cons

1. When buying unwarranted vehicles sold 'as seen', you can never be certain that you are not buying a car which has serious hidden problems because you cannot test it properly.

2. You buy under pressure, sometimes causing you to bid more than you originally intended.

3. There is no comeback on the vendors or the auctioneers, both of whom are protected by law if you buy a bad car sold 'as seen'. Furthermore, if you sell it on in bad or unroadworthy condition, whether intentionally or not, the buck stops with you. It becomes one hundred per cent your responsibility, so you are the one who ends up in serious trouble.

WANTED ADS

Pros

1. Good way of obtaining certain types of cars like rare sportscars or classics at under-the-market rate.

2. People who answer this type of advert are either generally unaware of their car's true market value (otherwise they would advertise it themselves) or are desperate for the money. Sometimes people can't be bothered with the hassle of selling a car themselves, they would rather have a dealer take it away for a quick cash sale than have the worry of dealing with the general public.

3. You get plenty of time to inspect cars properly buying them this way, so you know what you are getting.

Cons

Normally involves travelling quite a bit between vehicles, which again is costly in terms of time and money. That's why these adverts work out best as a means of obtaining special vehicles, like 'classics' or sportscars which have a healthy profit potential, to justify the expenses involved in running around.

BUYING 'TRADE-OFFS' FROM GARAGES

Pros

1. Vehicles can virtually always be bought under market value this way, at 'trade' price.

2. Normally you get a chance to inspect cars properly (often over a pit or up on a hoist) so you really know what you are getting. Usually the safest way of all to buy bargains.

3. Usually a choice of more than one car at any one location.

Cons

You buy on trade terms which means that you lose your rights under the Sale of Goods Act in regard to merchantable quality etc. i.e., you have virtually no comeback.

CHAPTER EIGHT

What Really Happens
At Auctions

Whether you are buying or selling cars at auction, it is essential that you have a good understanding of how they really work.

RUNNING UP

Probably the biggest of the two universal myths concerning auctions is that of 'running up'. Certainly, auctioneers can run up the price of a vehicle going under the hammer on non-existent bids ('bouncing them off a wall', as it is referred to in the trade) but only to within a bid or two of the reserve price below which the vehicle could not be sold anyway. No professional auctioneer will risk playing false bids off against a real bidder once the reserve has been reached. Think about it, the auctioneer only makes money if the car is sold and the way the commission rates work, the bidding would have to go on for a very long time before it made any real difference to his commission, so he has no motivation to risk losing that. Remember, all the auctioneer wants to do is to be sure of selling the car, getting his cut and shifting it out of the ring as soon as possible.

DEALERS' RINGS

The second myth is the so-called 'dealers' ring' in which a group of dealers supposedly get together and agree that only one of them will bid to keep the price down on selected vehicles in order to suppress the bid prices and then divide up the spoils afterwards. This is ridiculous. Whilst occasionally loose arrangements may be made between friends, there is no way that this can operate in the highly competitive auction ring of today where often motor traders are bidding against private members of the public for good cars. Now that so many private people attend auctions, 'dealers' rings' would virtually always be outbid by a member of the public or indeed other dealers operating outside these mythical rings. Indeed, I have yet to see any evidence of a 'dealers' ring' in operation in any of the hundreds of auctions that I have attended.

SECRET LANGUAGE

Right, having dispensed with myths, let's get down to the hard facts. What is essential to understand about auctions is what really goes on when a car is 'under the hammer' and how the bidding system works. For instance, there is a special language which is only understood by the auctioneers and the trade. Knowledge of this language separates the professionals from the punters, and indeed the average private person attending an auction is rarely, if ever, aware of its existence.

For example, when a car is under the hammer, an auctioneer will actually tell the trade roughly what they will be expected to pay within a hundred pounds or so *before* the bidding even starts, i.e. if a car has a reserve of £1,000 or thereabouts, the auctioneer will open with *"Okay, where shall we start then? £800, £900?"* He will then probably move off with a first bid at about £600, whether it is a real bid or simply 'bounced off the wall'. Now we come to the interesting bit. Auctioneers are generally highly experienced valuers of cars. If, through his experience, the auctioneer thinks the car is overpriced at its reserve, he may tend to quote a figure around £200 less in the hopes of attracting interest which might eventually build up to the point where somebody pays the reserve. On the other hand, if he feels that the car is undervalued, he may do the opposite and even quote over the reserve. As the bidding climbs to within a couple of bids of the actual reserve price, he will very quickly interject *"against the owners now"* which tells the trade that it will now only take a couple of bids to buy the car. If, however, the bidding is a long way from the reserve price, he may say something like *"miles away"*, or *"long way to go"* in between bids, but this will be done so quickly and deftly that only the experienced trader will pick it up. Of course, sometimes the bidding goes on over the reserve price when there is some keen competition for the car. When it has actually gone over the reserve price, the auctioneer will interject something like *"all your own money now"* or even *"all your own bids"*; then the trade knows that the last bid will actually buy the car.

Should a car be entered in the sale without a reserve, or with a very low reserve relative to its normal value, the auctioneer will often say something like *"the car is here to be sold"*. The trade then knows that this car can definitely be bought if they want it. Here is another example of the secret language which can prove extremely useful to you. If the last bid is too far away from the reserve price for the car to be sold, the auctioneer will mumble quickly under his breath something like *"bought in"* which tells the trade that it wasn't actually sold but if they are interested, they can come along and put another bid on it after the auction.

CAR PARK SALES

'Car park sales' can often prove a good way of buying cars because you sometimes get the chance to test drive the vehicle round the car park and also, as the car has, at that point, passed through the auction system, the auctioneers will actually volunteer the reserve price, simply because, if they don't do so, there is very little chance of you buying the car. Remember, even if the car is bought *after* it has passed through the ring, the auctioneers are still entitled to their commission providing it is sold via their introduction.

Sometimes dealers arrange to buy cars from each other later outside the auction grounds because the vendor is prepared to accept less for cash owing to the fact that he will not have to pay the auctioneer's commission fee. Naturally the auctioneers don't like this practice and may in some cases even be able to sue for their commission if they can prove their case. For this reason, most 'car park sales' like this between dealers are done extremely discreetly! Unfortunately, it is a fact of life that the best cars nearly always get purchased in the ring, so it will generally be only by a stroke of good fortune that you end up with the chance to buy a bargain like this. However, should a car in which you are interested not make its money under the hammer, it is always worthwhile to go and ask the auctioneers what the reserve price is. Then you can either offer to meet this or go and stand by the car until the owner comes with the key to collect it, because you can always go back to the auctioneers after you have made a full inspection of the car, or decide not to as the case may be.

HOW TO BID

Successful bidding at auction is all about strategy and psychology. It is important to complete all of your inspection of the vehicle before it goes anywhere near the ring. Never let other dealers see you looking too hard at a car just as it goes in to be sold. If you are spotted, it gives the opposition time to reassess the vehicle knowing there may be serious competition, particularly if you are known by reputation for paying good money for certain types of vehicle. Do all of your checking and inspection out in the car park and then, armed with the knowledge of exactly how much you want to pay having taken into consideration any money you feel you will have to spend on the car, plus a little bit of leeway for luck, pick your position in the ring. (This is where your notepad concerning faults relating to particular vehicles and lot numbers will become invaluable.)

Give some consideration to where you stand or sit in the auction ring. I believe that the best place to stand is well back in the crowd somewhere, where the competition finds it difficult to keep an eye on you, but always choose a spot where you will be able to maintain eye contact with the auctioneer when you start bidding. When the bidding starts on the vehicle, stay cool. Never, whatever you do, start putting your hand up straightaway. The auctioneer can only take bids from two people at a time, so wait as long as you possibly can. Personally, my own method was to wait until the auctioneer raised his hammer for the first time, calling for last bids. At this point, he will usually say something like *"Any more?"*. The secret then is to raise your arm very quickly and then put it down again as soon as he has seen you. Forget the nods and winks on your first bid, it is essential that he sees you, otherwise you may lose the car, and, as you have not been bidding throughout the time that the car has been under the hammer, the trade will not be watching you. Once the auctioneer knows you are in the market for the car, he will keep looking your way for further bids which can then be done by the proverbial nods and winks, which are just sufficient for him to see but no one else.

There are various strategies for wearing down the opposition if you are bidding against other people. One method I used to employ was to keep bidding away and then feign disinterest, allowing my opponent to think he was going to get the car and then, just as the auctioneer was raising the hammer for the last time, I would quickly interject another bid. By doing this two or three times, I have usually found it possible to break the nerve of the toughest opponent.

CHAPTER NINE

DIRTY TRICKS DEPARTMENT

This is such a vast subject that, as you can imagine, a whole book could be written about it in itself. Even then there would be some gems missing! Please bear in mind though that the vast majority of the motor trade is completely honest and would never resort to any of the following dastardly deeds. However, inevitably, there is a roguish element in any walk of life and it would certainly surprise me if you didn't encounter a few dirty tricks throughout your motor dealing career.

So here are some basic ones to watch out for when buying cars at auction.

1. Always suspect a car that is locked in the car park whilst others are unlocked. Generally it means one of two things: either the owner doesn't want anyone to find that the clutch or brake pedals are soft or there is something under the bonnet (usually released from inside the passenger compartment) that he doesn't want you to see, e.g. a duff engine, bodged welding or accident damage.

2. Normally, the windscreen ticket giving information on the car is placed under the wiper. Beware of a car without a windscreen ticket. It means the owner doesn't want to put it on until the last minute so that you shouldn't find out something, like the fact that the MOT is short or that the car is listed as a Hackney Carriage or was once an insurance write-off.

3. Beware if you see the owner sitting beside the auction driver when the car is driven into the ring. He is there to make sure

that the driver does not make obvious some fault, i.e. first gear might be missing. Likewise, suspect any automatic rolling into the ring with the lever set at '1' or '2' instead of 'D' if the owner has been hanging about when the auction driver got in.

4. It is not unknown for the unscrupulous to switch the middle two plug leads around on a car whilst they are pretending to inspect the engine if they want to buy it. They would do this if they had been at the auction site earlier in the day to see the car driven in. Knowing it to be all right, they sabotage it like this so that it will be running rough when it goes under the hammer and the price will be kept down. Counteract this by learning the firing order of vehicles which you most frequently buy so that just by looking at them, you can tell whether the leads are wrong.

5. A favourite psychological trick employed by dealers is to lift the bonnet and wait for the engine to start. When it does, they laugh derisively or slam the bonnet with a comment like *"That's the end of that story!"* in order to put you off buying it when really they are satisfied everything is alright. Don't let other dealers intimidate or influence you.

6. Suspect anyone who hangs around a car in a car park and either praises it (obviously the seller trying to up the price) or conversely, runs it down (a hopeful buyer). Make your own decisions.

7. An old trick is to put an incorrect model badge on the rear of a car to make it appear a more desirable buy. This is often done in connection with jamming the bonnet catch in order to prevent anyone from discovering the ploy. Never take badges for granted, always check yourself.

8. In the case of older cars in particular, watch out for five-speed gear box knobs placed on four-speed boxes, especially on cars that are in change-over years like 1982 Ford Escorts. If you get into an early five-speed car, always attempt to select fifth gear to check it is there.

9. Watch for glued down carpets or floor mats covering nasty holes in the floor pans. The same rule goes for boots in the case of older cars where a glued down carpet or lining often conceals a terminal corrosion problem.

10. When inspecting a vehicle's engine bay, always look for loose wires that should be connected to the engine, especially the oil light lead. When a car is going into the ring, a lot of people look at the speedo to check the mileage and if the oil pressure is low, this is when the light will show. Many oil light leads conveniently 'fall off' the engine. The same goes for temperature gauge wires. A more subtle, but thankfully rarer, trick is when the oil light bulb is removed from the dashboard and sprayed with black paint before being replaced. This way, although it comes on when the key is first turned, it glows so dimly on tickover that it is hard to see in daylight. This one is hard to detect; make a habit of looking hard at all oil lights!

11. An old trick for disguising worn big end bearing rattles in an engine is to deliberately retard the ignition timing. Beware of any engine which seems reluctant to rev freely or stutters at high r.p.m.

12. Some unscrupulous people mix iron filings into body filler to make detection with a magnet more difficult. However, the pudding still feels warmer than the steel around it. So, if in doubt, pull up your sleeve and test the suspect area with your wrist, just on the point where you would check your own pulse, which is particularly sensitive to temperature differences.

Don't let other dealers intimidate or influence you.
– p. 70

CHAPTER TEN

How To Prepare A Car For Sale

The object of successful motor dealing is to turn over cars as easily and quickly as possible. Whether you are dealing within the trade or retailing them to the public, the more trouble you take in initial cleaning up and proper preparation, the faster they will sell and, in turn, the more money you will be making. A common fault with motor traders is that they simply don't appear to realise this. Surprisingly, few of them really take the trouble to make the best of a car and present it nicely. The importance of proper preparation cannot be overemphasised. I can think of friends of mine, non-motor traders, who will take months to sell a car which I could guarantee to sell within a week simply because they won't prepare it properly. That is the difference between professionals and amateurs.

BODYWORK

This subject is too large to go into in great detail (after all, bodywork apprentices work for years to gain the necessary knowledge) but I can pass on some useful tips.

1. If possible, when dealing with the banger end of the market, as I have mentioned in an earlier chapter, avoid buying cars that need paint in the middle of panels as these are much harder to touch up successfully with an aerosol than edges of panels such as door bottoms or wheel arches. Obviously if you are purchasing more expensive cars then you have to take into consideration the cost of respraying entire panels properly.

2. Most metallic paints are impossible to match with aerosol cans. So again, unless a professional respray of the panels concerned is cost effective in relation to your profit margin, avoid buying metallic cars which need any major attention.

3. Try to avoid spraying aerosol paint on a damp day. It will leave a white bloom on the finish which is impossible to remove. (I think this is because the paint picks up moisture particles on its way from the can nozzle to the car panel.)

4. Likewise try not to use aerosols on a cold day if possible. If it is totally unavoidable, then keep the can warm inside the house until the very last moment before you start to spray. If possible, warm the panel first by holding a powerful inspection lamp or hairdryer close to the area which is to be sprayed; **not** *while you are actually spraying, of course, as this could be dangerous, and* **don't** *use a* **naked flame** *whatever you do, because paint is highly flammable and aerosols are explosive!*

5. When mixing up body filler, I have found that it is possible to use up to four times the recommended amount of hardener to speed up the process of it setting. *Don't do this with fibreglass*, though, and remember, *never* use body filler to repair damage or corrosion to any **structurally important** part of the car as this could lead to criminal prosecution.

6. The best way of getting a good finish on body filler for an amateur (as opposed to a bodywork professional) is to build up layers of it a little at a time rather than try to put it all on at once. Then when you have rubbed it down, mix up a little more and fill the tiny air holes with the end of a knife blade. You can use a very strong mixture for this which will cure quickly.

7. If time is short, don't bother to use primer over filler; simply spray the top coat straight on. Once you have used a primer, you will have to spend far more time rubbing it back to get it smooth. The use of an aerosol can is just a bodge really, so there is no point in pretending that you are doing a professional job.

8. When rubbing down, do it in three stages. Start with 60 or 80 grade paper to get it roughly right, smooth it out with 120 or 180 grade and finish with a 1,000 or 1,200 grade (this is suitable for rubbing down the paint as well). Then 'T Cut' it.

9. When spraying, do lots of very light coats and count to approximately 15 seconds between each. If you concentrate a lot of paint in one go, it will cause runs which will take much longer to put right in the end.

10. If you are trying to touch up a stone chip or small scratch, try to avoid spraying at all; you will end up with a much larger blemish. Simply spray the colour into the can cap and apply it with a small brush or even the end of a matchstick in the case of a small stone chip. If you are patient, you can build the paint up until it makes the blemish considerably less visible.

11. You can remove 'over-spray' on glass, rubber or chrome with wire-wool pan-cleaner pads dipped in warm water. When spraying fiddly bits, I have often found it quicker to rub off the over-spray like this rather than bother to mask the area with tape. Try and do this as soon as possible after spraying before the paint gets too hard.

12. In certain situations, it is quite useful to spray rubber trim and fiddly bits with WD40 before you start spraying around the area. Usually, provided you don't leave it too long until after you have finished painting, you can simply wipe off the precoated items and remove any over-spray instantly. Obviously, be careful that you don't spray any WD40 on to areas which you *do* wish to paint!

13. If you need to cut back paint faster than you can achieve with 'T Cut' and you can't get hold of any 1200 paper, use a metal polish like 'Autosol'. It brings off the worst quickly and then you can finish with the 'T Cut'.

14. Don't spray on a windy day if you wear glasses or contact lenses; paint travels a lot further than you think!

15. When you are spraying and rubbing down body filler, for goodness sake wear a mask and give your throat and lungs a chance!

All this is a bit dull so I must tell you a funny story which happens to be absolutely true. A car dealer I once heard about had an old banger with holes in its outer sills. He wanted to fill them in a hurry so he stuffed a whole packet of household pan-cleaning wire-wool pads into them and then filled over with pudding (very naughty!). When rubbed down and sprayed over, the job looked fine. This was during the summer and there had been a fine spell for a few days. However, just when a punter arrived to look at the car, it began to rain. On completion of the test drive, they alighted from the car to discover to their amazement it was foaming bubbles furiously from every oriface because the soap in the pan cleaning pads had become saturated! Never at a loss, the dealer calmly turned to the totally astonished punter and said *"Oh yes, that's another point I forgot to mention, this was BL's experimental self-cleaning model!"* Needless to say, he didn't sell the car. Serves him right!

HOW TO CLEAN UP A CAR WELL

The object of the exercise is to make a vehicle look like a genuine clean car, not a 'tart' that has just been toshed up for sale. Things like tyre black are right out. Punters will spot that a mile away, whether in auction or retail and run in the opposite direction as quickly as possible. The way to do it properly is as follows:-

1. Having done all the touching up and spraying etc., give the car a really good wash including scrubbing the side walls of the tyres and wheels.

2. If the paintwork is shabby or faded, give the car a good going over with colour restorer and then wax it.

3. Give the interior of the car a really good sweeping out, empty all the ashtrays, rubbish between the seats etc. including the glove box compartment and the shelves. Then use a

powerful vacuum cleaner to finish the job. Repair any tears in seats with a simple bit of glueing or sewing. In the case of older cars, it is sometimes acceptable to fit seat covers.

4. Cover holes in grotty carpets with a cheap set of mats. To make dashboards and all interior plastic or vinyl surfaces look much brighter, use a silicone spray like 'Cockpit Shine'. This can even be applied to some seats if they are vinyl or leather covered. It makes a tremendous difference to the interior. Always leave the doors open and wear a mask when spraying it though!

5. If there is a nasty odour in the car, leave a car deodoriser in for a few days but use two at once and then take them out on the day of the sale. I used to keep two or three of these going permanently and swap them from one car to another two days at a time.

6. Pull all those silly 'My other car is a Lamborghini' and 'Save the Ostrich' type stickers off the rear window and then polish all glass inside and out of the car, including rear view mirrors and instruments, with one of the modern and convenient spray glass cleaners. You would be surprised how few people in the trade realise the difference this can make to even the most grotty car. Glass makes up about 25% of the total visual area of a car and psychologically when people are sitting in a car, if they can see out through the windscreen clearly, it always puts them in a positive frame of mind.

7. On the average car, you should usually aim to spend about three quarters of an hour cleaning up the engine compartment. If you have a local steam cleaner, that's great, but otherwise get rid of all the oily goo on the engine with some sort of degreasing agent like 'Gunk'. Always remember, *it can be very dangerous to use petrol or paraffin to clean an engine!* If you must use either, for goodness sake disconnect the battery negative first, or at the very least, take the ignition keys out. I knew someone who set himself on fire once doing this job and it was not a pretty sight! A spark from a battery terminal is all it takes! So keep metal objects

away from the battery if you must do it this way. *(Preferably take the battery out when doing this job.)*

8. When the engine compartment is dry, tidy it up, generally pushing all loose wires and bits and pieces into their correct place. If the radiator is looking a bit manky, take a can of gloss black aerosol and, masking off the front of the car with a bit of cardboard, spray over the top of it. This little trick often brightens up the engine compartment considerably. The smallest detail can make a tremendous difference. Sometimes it is worth replacing that rusy old radiator cap with a new one (only £2). It all helps to create the impression of a well-looked-after car.

9. Clean the boot out really well and replace the carpet with a better one from a scrapyard if it's tatty. If it smells damp, dry it out by leaving the bootlid open on a good day, or putting a deodoriser in the boot for a few days.

10. If you have time, it is always a good idea to run over the salient chrome work and trim with a product like 'Autosol'. Very few vehicles these days actually have any chrome work but on the older cars, this helps quite a lot.

11. Finally, always make sure to open all the doors and check that each door surround is absolutely clean. If you are short of time, just do this on the driver's door, paying particular attention to what he will see climbing in and out of the car.

All this preparation may seem like a lot of bother but, believe me, if you have taken the trouble to do this to a basically clean car, you will be rewarded by finding that it sells much more quickly and makes a better price at auction.

Cleaning up cars is especially important if you are retailing; a bit of extra time spent in toshing up a motor saves a lot of time later hanging around showing it to various different people who go away and never come back. The truth is that most cars are in such a horrible state when people look at them that when they find a clean one, they are so overwhelmed they are almost bound to buy it and often end up paying more than they originally intended to. If you are not sure of your ability as a salesman, then this preparation is all the more important largely because the car will sell itself. It is only lazy motor traders who can't be bothered to take this sort of trouble in the first place that end up waiting for hours for people who don't buy the car anyway, simply because it doesn't look good enough. These are the guys that you always hear moaning about the so-called 'time wasters'.

If you want an example of how important cleaning a vehicle can be in terms of adding to the value, try this one. A friend of mine bought a five-series BMW in a Midlands auction a while back. It was an HP company repossession car. It was absolutely filthy inside and out and he bought it for about £1,550. He spent a whole day cleaning it from top to bottom and the following week, he put it back in the same auction. It made £5,700! He cleared about £4,000 after auctioneer's fees, not a bad little tickle for a day's car cleaning!

Lastly, always remember that if you are going to deal in more expensive cars, it is essential to find yourself a good, professional car valet. There will come a point where you simply don't have time to clean each individual car up to a high standard yourself, besides which, very few of us actually match the expertise of a well equipped and experienced professional valet. Once you find one, try hard to develop a good working relationship with him, because there will definitely be times when you want him to clean up a car speedily in order to pull off a quick deal!

"Oh yes, that's another point I forgot to mention, this was BL's experimental self-cleaning model!"
– p. 76

CHAPTER ELEVEN

HOW TO ADVERTISE A CAR

When advertising vehicles, it always pays to give some thought to which magazines or newspapers are most suitable for your needs. A particular make or model of vehicle may sell better through one newspaper or magazine than another. For instance, if you are selling run-of-the-mill bread-and-butter cars, then your best bet is to advertise locally, either in a newspaper (preferably on a Friday or Saturday, because most people go car hunting at the weekend) or in one of those special weekly car magazines which are full of photographs of cars for sale in your area, like *AutoTrader*. Personally, I have found this to be more successful than newspapers for selling cars locally, because, now this type of magazine has become established, most people who are seriously looking for a car in their area will buy a copy at the local newsagent every week until they find the right vehicle. As an advertising method, it has three main advantages over conventional newspapers. Firstly, it generally works out much cheaper, as the insertion fee, which gives you a week or a fortnight's exposure in the magazine including a free photograph, costs about the same as just one day in a newspaper. Secondly, the fact that people can see the car in a photograph encourages them to ring. Thirdly, these magazines normally give you a more generous and flexible wordage allowance than newspapers, which helps considerably. For these reasons I would always recommend this type of magazine as first choice for local advertising.

Should you be selling a special interest vehicle, such as a rare sportscar or classic vehicle, then you may very well sell it more quickly and indeed at a better price, by advertising it nationally.

Remember, the sort of people who are looking for such vehicles are always prepared to travel much further afield. Depending on what sort of vehicle it is, there is a wide choice of effective national advertising available. *The Exchange & Mart* is an obvious one, for instance. *The Sunday Times* can be a useful advertising medium for rarer vehicles under the 'Collectors Cars' or 'Performance Cars' sections. You could also consider special interest magazines such as *Classic & Sportscar*. My advice is, if you have a special vehicle, take a browse through the shelves of your nearest newsagent and give serious thought as to which is likely to prove the most suitable selling magazine.

HOW TO PLACE A GOOD ADVERT

The object of successful advertising is to attract potential punters to your car as quickly as possible by making them pick yours out of a page full of adverts for similar vehicles, whilst at the same time, minimising the risk of getting yourself into trouble with the Department of Fair Trading/Advertising Standards etc. I can best demonstrate this by showing you an example of firstly a bad, and then a good, advert for exactly the same vehicle. This kind of advert is the type which appears in the small ads section of any local newspaper.

A bad advert

Rover MG Metro 1300 J-reg. Immaculate condition throughout. MOT'd. No rust. Stereo. New battery. Real bargain. £3,000 - Knockingwell 25743 (trade).

So, you might ask, what is wrong with that? Well, quite a number of things.

1. Never start an advert with the make of a car like *Ford* or *Rover*. It is a waste of valuable word space and, more importantly, slows up the process of a potential punter who is looking for a particular model from finding your car. He knows he wants a Metro or a Sierra or whatever and he already knows who makes them; he doesn't need to be told. So always start an advert with the model first, i.e. Sierra, or in this case, Metro.

The only exception to this rule is when advertising rare, prestige or sports cars in which case it is an advantage to start with the maker first, i.e. 'Lotus Esprit' rather than 'Esprit Lotus', because it makes them stand out better in a page full of ordinary cars.

2. Putting *'J-reg'* in this case was a mistake. The car is 1992, J-reg could be late 1991. Always quote the most advantageous of the two choices; in this case 1992. Conversely, if it were a late 1991, mention only 'J-reg'.

3. Never, under any circumstances, use words like *immaculate* or *very good condition*. When advertising a really nice car, never go beyond words like 'attractive, tidy, smart' or 'worth seeing', because these refer strictly to appearance only. If the car develops a mechanical problem later, for instance, after you have sold it, at least no one can accuse you of misrepresenting it in the advert. However, they could feasibly do so if you put 'immaculate', because this can be interpreted as referring to overall condition, including mechanical condition, rather than just the appearance.

4. Putting the word *'MOT'd'* was a chronic mistake. It could mean that it only had a week of ticket left. A major selling point is a long MOT, so in this case it should have said 'Year's MOT' or 'New MOT'.

5. *'No rust'*. This one is positively suicidal! Technically speaking, you couldn't even say this about a new car. There will always be some rust in a steel body, however slight, so never even consider this one or 'rust free' either.

6. Putting just the word *'stereo'* is not enough. It isn't just any old stereo; the car has an expensive, well-known make so why not say so? It looks far more impressive.

7. *'New battery'*. A complete waste of space. This doesn't convey anything good about the car at all. No one is going to have their purchase decision influenced by whether the car has a new battery or not. If it were a new exhaust system, it might be different. Learn to recognise those things which you

should mention on a car which have been recently replaced and indeed those that are not worth mentioning. For instance, no one really cares whether a car has had a new timing chain replaced. On the other hand, people are interested to hear that it has had a new exhaust system simply because they recognise that this is an item which needs reasonably frequent replacement and is relatively expensive.

8. *'Real bargain'*. This is too tacky for words. It is far more likely to drive people away than attract them. If you are going to say things like that, say 'Priced for quick sale'. This gives the impression that the vehicle is, in fact, a real bargain because the vendor is prepared to accept a realistic price in order to effect a quick sale.

9. *'£3,000'*. Never use round numbers; always end a price under a price break, as they say in the retail trade, i.e. £2,995. If you quote a round number, potential buyers tend to think that you won't come down from a price which they may be feeling is more than they wish to pay when reading the advert. However, if they come along and look at the car, they probably think that they are going to get it for, let's say, £2,700, but because it is so clean and well presented, you can probably hold it at around £2,800 which is what you are expecting to get in the first place. However, the point is that if you had put it in at £3,000, that very same punter might never have even picked up the phone in the first instance.

It is not only what you say, but the order in which it is stated that matters. The secret is to get the most important information across in the first line so that the interested party gets enough of the right gen instantly to hold his attention and read further. This is an example of how the advert for that very same vehicle should have been written:

A good advert

'Metro MG 1300. 1992. New MOT, 27,000 miles. Very attractive car in metallic dark blue. Full service history. Panasonic stereo. Sunroof. £2,995 - Knockingwell 25743 (trade).'

84

See how the car comes across now as a really genuine-sounding and interesting vehicle. A potential buyer has learned so much more information about it before he has even picked up the phone. With an advert like this, you can already mentally picture the vehicle because you know its colour. It sounds like the sort of car which has been carefully looked after by a doting previous owner.

If you have more space, you can make a vehicle sound really interesting and attractive by picking out all the best aspects about it without mentioning those things which detract from it, just like most estate agents have been doing with property adverts for years! For instance, you might have just an average Jaguar XJ6 which is neither better nor worse than any other but you can make it sound especially attractive by mentioning those aspects of the car which make it the luxury vehicle that it is; and even though most of these benefits are standard, this still makes your vehicle sound particularly alluring.

For instance:

Jaguar XJ6 3.6 1990. Recent MOT. Finished in Brooklands green with tan leather interior. Alloy wheels. Air conditioning. Electric windows. Pioneer stereo cassette. Stainless steel exhaust. A realistically priced example of this luxury prestige car, £2,495 - Knockingwell 25743 (trade).

If you look at this advert, it appears as though you have made a lot of extravagant claims about the car but actually you haven't at all. Nothing stated could possibly be construed as a false statement. To take an extreme case by way of example, mentioning the fact that it is finished in Brooklands green with a tan leather interior actually doesn't tell you anything about the condition of the car, because the fact is that the Brooklands green bodywork may be slightly shabby through neglect and the tan leather may have seen better days. It would have been a very different story if you had stated something like *immaculate bodywork finished in Brooklands green* or *spotless tan leather interior*. The advert would look no better for doing this but you would have put yourself at risk unnecessarily.

85

SPORTSCARS

In the case of sportscars, it is often possible to build an image around the car which will attract the right sort of person to it without having to say very much or possibly anything about the *actual* car which you have up for sale. For instance:

> **E-type Jaguar 3.8 series 1/2. Bright red. Wire wheels. Last of the real performance E-types. 0-60 in 7 secs. 140 mph+. Not for the faint-hearted! £23,995 - Knockingwell 25743 (trade).**

See how this advert helps to create an exciting impression of the car. Everything stated in it is true. Performance figures have been proved by road testers and officially recorded. And by saying *'not for the faint-hearted'*, you are, of course, attracting the very sort of person who wants to buy this type of vehicle. An advert like this can be very useful when you are selling a car which is perhaps a little tatty appearance wise, i.e. although it is safe, sound and serviceable, it could perhaps benefit from a re-spray and the interior being re-done. Because of considerations like these, you don't wish to make outlandish claims about the car, but at the same time you need to attract punters to come and see it.

Unfortunately, sportscars often suffer much harder lives than the run-of-the-mill family cars and this is why it is often safer to use this method of advertising. Also, due to the fact they are generally produced in lower volume than family cars, they often have inherent design faults which are never properly rectified by the manufacturer. Anyone who has driven the old type (1960s) Lotus Elans will know what superb little cars they were, but they were also about as reliable as a long-range weather forecast! Triumph Stags were fine cars too, but were renowned for engine problems if not properly serviced and so on. Obviously this is not true in every case, but is worth bearing in mind.

Sometimes you can make a special interest car sound more exciting by employing what is referred to as 'advertising puff'. This is really a statement which is clearly not meant to be taken literally but, nevertheless, creates an impression all the same and hopefully creates more interest in the advert. An example of this might be:

Renault 5 Turbo 1990. Tuned engine. Racing red. Shattering performance. 0-60 in 7.5 secs. Pilot's licence essential to drive this four-wheeled ballistic missile! £2,495 - Knockingwell 25743 (trade).

Obviously the statement *'pilot's licence essential'* and so on is not meant to be taken literally, it is simply meant to add a bit of zip to the ad. Perhaps this is rather an exaggerated example but it gives you the general idea of what 'advertising puff' is. It should be used with caution, though; make sure that the 'puff' cannot be construed as a literal statement.

One final and important point. If you advertise a vehicle for motor trading purposes, i.e. to make a profit through it, under the Trades Description Act you must make this clear in your advert. The rules concerning how this is done do seem to vary slightly from area to area. Generally speaking, you have to put the word 'trade' in the advert after the telephone number or at least somewhere in the advert. In some cases, and in some newspapers, they will allow you to put in something like 'dealer facilities available' which shows that you are obviously in the trade. In some types of publication, the designation 'T' after the advert is enough. Be sure to check the ruling in your local area before advertising. If in doubt, contact your local Trading Standards Office through the nearest Citizens Advice Bureau. Some people believe that putting the word 'Trade' in an advert discourages punters from ringing but if your advert is good enough, you should always generate sufficient interest. Remember, if the Trading Standards people catch you advertising as if you are a private person, you could be liable to a heavy fine which is probably the last thing you need!

COMMONLY USED ADVERT ABBREVIATIONS

FSH	Full Service History
VGC	Very Good Condition
ONO	Or Nearest Offer
WHY?	What Have You? (to P/X etc.)
T & T	Taxed and Tested
RM	Recorded Mileage
PAS	Power Assisted Steering
O/D	Overdrive
LSD	Limited Slip Differential
LWB	Long Wheel Base
SWB	Short Wheel Base
W/W	Wide Wheels/Wire Wheels (in case of classics)
ESR	Electric Sun Roof
BHP	Brake Horse Power
SS/Exhaust	Stainless Steel Exhaust
LHD	Left Hand Drive
FWD	Four Wheel Drive
CL	Central Locking
AB	Air Bag
ABS	Anti-lock Braking System
A/C	Air Conditioning

CHAPTER TWELVE

How to Sell a Car
From an Advertisement

Before I begin this subject, I would like to make it quite clear that I regard the sales techniques required to sell vehicles from newspaper adverts as being entirely different from those needed for selling cars from garage premises. Therefore, I am going to discuss these two forms of selling separately.

When you are attempting to sell a car through an advert, it is vital for your financial survival that you sell it fast. If it sticks around in the paper week after week, you have progressively less chance, not only of getting a good price for it, but of selling it at all, because people will think that there is some reason why it has not sold. Therefore, it is necessary to employ certain sales techniques which will give you the best chance of ensuring a rapid sale because you cannot afford to be stuck with a landmark. On the other hand, as a retailer selling from garage premises, you have other considerations to bear in mind such as establishing a good reputation and gaining long term customer confidence. In this case then, it is necessary to deal with people in an entirely different way in order to be successful. However, if you are fortunate enough to be in the financial position to set yourself up as a retailer like this, then you can also afford to take this longer term view.

UNDERSTANDING PEOPLE

The most important thing to understand about selling cars to people is how they feel and react when they are looking at them.

Human nature is a contrary and fickle thing. The fact is that when someone is thinking about buying a car, they are balancing on a knife edge of indecision. They want to buy the car, but, subsconsciously, when faced with the actual decision of having to part with their money, they love to find an excuse not to go through with it.

There is nothing a punter loves better than to turn up and discover that even though your particular car is a perfect example of what he has been looking for, he has a viable excuse not to buy it. You know the sort of thing, a chap comes to look at a car, finds it is exactly what he is looking for, the best he has seen so far. One half of him feels very pleased, but the other half starts to ring panic bells. He is now actually confronted with having to part with his hard earned dosh. Just as he begins to sweat, his wife pulls the plug on it by informing him that she has just realised the vehicle is no good for them after all because the rear doors are too narrow to squeeze her fat mother through; he is saved by the bell! This gives him the excuse he needs not to buy it, and the chance to grumble to his wife all the way home about missing the best bargain yet. Half of him feels disappointed, but the other half feels extremely relieved at the same time.

Even better, what people really love is to turn up just too late and miss a real bargain. This gives them the chance to moan about 'the one that got away' later on in the pub that evening. Seriously though, it is important to realise that when people are looking at cars, they are undergoing considerable mental turmoil; if you can get your head around that concept, then you are halfway to success already.

SELLING CARS THROUGH NEWSPAPER ADVERTS

Having accepted the fact that people are balancing on a knife-edge of indecision, then selling cars is all about helping them step off it and make the decision in your favour. In the case of selling cars through adverts, this has to be done swiftly and surely for the reasons which I have already mentioned. In order to achieve this, it is necessary to relax people and yet put them under subtle pressure at the same time. This sounds impossible doesn't it? It isn't, believe me, as you will soon see.

PUNTERS ON THE PHONE

The first thing to disregard is high pressure sales methods. This is the last thing that is going to make anyone buy a car. When someone buys a car, he is really buying the man who sells it as well. The more relaxed and quietly confident you appear to be, 'laid back' if you like, the more chance you will have of a successful sale. For instance, when someone first rings up and asks about a car, don't push a lot of sales chat at him. Just sound genuine and friendly and give him the impression from the start that there has already been quite a number of enquiries in response to your advert. Whatever you do, don't allow him to feel that he is the only person to show an interest, this will worry him. Any potential purchaser will always feel a lot more confident if he thinks that he is not the only one after the vehicle.

Nine times out of ten, people will open the conversation with something like *"Have you still got the car?"*. Resist replying keenly with a simple *"Yes I have"*. Instead, reply rather hesitantly, with something like *"Er, yes, well it is still here is at the moment"* and hold back rather, don't rush at him; remain cool, but cheerful and polite.

When the chap is on the phone, let him ask the questions and if he is having trouble thinking of any, subtly help him along. Never come out with obvious things like *"the bodywork is really superb"* (assuming that this applies, of course). Rather, go in at an indirect angle by saying something like *"Oh yes, I know what it's like trying to find a decent, reasonably priced car these days, so few of them are really clean"*. He will then be forced to reply with something like *"Oh, is yours really nice then?"* to which you are then able to reply in surprised tones, as if by now you are used to your old 'shed' being regarded as an exceptional example, *"Oh yes, superb for its age"*. The use of subtle techniques such as these result in a potential buyer feeling that he has stumbled upon a bargain rather than been force-fed sales chat.

91

HOW TO DEAL WITH PEOPLE

When someone comes to view a car, always hold back on the sales chat to start with. Start a conversation about anything and everything else but the car itself. If at all possible, start talking to his wife, or, if she has come to look at the car, start talking to the husband, but whatever you do, don't start talking about the car because this is exactly what they expect you to do. By casually engaging them in conversation, you will immediately throw them off their guard and help to melt their defences. The more laid back and quietly confident you appear to be, the quicker they will respond to you. The subtle trick is to create a relaxed atmosphere between yourselves and the prospective buyers as quickly as possible, but, at the same time, as they look around the car, ensure that they notice all of its best points in the least obvious way possible.

When selling a car then, put yourself in the punter's shoes. Think how you react yourself when viewing a vehicle, the sort of things you want to hear and the sort of things you don't want to hear. Present everything to a prospective buyer on the phone and indeed when he comes to view the car, from his angle. Even if he is really thick, always make him feel that he has found out the salient things that he needs to know about the car himself, make him feel good, and even clever, and he will probably buy the car!

An important reason for encouraging the impression that you have received considerable response to your advert is that this appeals to that aspect of human nature which is sometimes referred to as 'one-upmanship'. People want to feel that, although there are lots of other people after the car, they, in some miraculous way, will be able to pip them all at the post by getting there first. This aspect of human nature can be used very much to your advantage and it will often help you effect a quick sale.

By offering to hold the car for an interested party until a certain time, you can in the most subtle way put him under pressure before he even comes to look at it. When he does turn up you can add fuel to his enthusiasm by dropping little quips:

"I never realised just how popular this model was until I put this one up for sale! I suppose it must be because really clean ones are difficult to find". A bold statement like this puts you in an all-win situation because the punter will either have only just started looking for a car, in which case you will have already worried him that he may not find a better one, or he has been to see and subsequently rejected quite a few rough ones already, in which case your properly prepared example will entice him. However, a remark like this will also please him because he thinks he is the first one to view the vehicle and the fact that so many other people appear to think it is a bargain will help to persuade him that it is.

The most important point I am attempting to get across here is that successful selling depends on remaining calm, laid back almost to the point of being detached. This is the last thing that anyone expects to find in a car salesman, and, providing you remain polite and cheerful throughout, without resorting to sickly charm, you will always find that your potential purchaser relaxes quickly which, although he doesn't realise it, makes him vulnerable to your highly refined sales tactics. There is never any need to put a customer under pressure, because he is already under pressure from his own human nature. The desire to pip his fellow man to the post by buying a bargain before someone else is more than enough pressure for anyone!

Pressure is all a matter of perception; if he realises that he is under pressure, the punter may react negatively by not buying the car. Interestingly, he doesn't recognise the pressure of his own human nature, so, although he can immediately recognise any pressure put upon him by a salesman because he is expecting it, he doesn't identify the stress he is putting *himself* under. This is the reason why a highly successful car salesman always relaxes his customers, because they immediately relate to him and come to regard him as the 'good guy' in a stressful situation, because he is calming them down, rather than adding to their problems. The salesman of course knows differently.

In my experience, it is seldom necessary to drop more than the exact amount that you allowed for haggling when you priced the car. If you can manage to keep your nerve and give the impression that you really aren't that bothered, which indicates that you are confident that lots of other people will buy the vehicle, you should always be able to out-psych the buyer. Often you won't have to drop much at all. Generally speaking, it balances out; you may have to drop a little more than you want on one car, but then on another, you will probably be able to hold your price.

Should you be having a particular problem with a really tough bargainer, it is not a bad idea to have a go at 'thought transference', i.e. putting words into his mouth. For instance, let's say he has offered you £1,250 and he won't budge but the lowest sum that you can accept to make a decent 'shout' on the motor is £1,400. You could say something like *"Yes, well, I know there are a couple of others in the paper for less than the £1,400 that I want, but as you say, you never see them as clean as this normally. I can always bear your offer in mind but the thing is, someone else is coming in a minute and he did sound very keen on the phone, so, if it's alright by you, I think I will wait to see what he comes up with first."* Now, the fact is, the chap never *did* say the car was clean but you have now transferred the thought to him and started him worrying that he is going to lose a good car, the likes of which he probably won't find again for a long time, for the sake of a few quid. In other words, you have given him the excuse he needs to step off the knife-edge of indecision and in your favour.

The golden rule of thumb here is that if someone turns up and in the first few moments says something like *"It's very clean, isn't it?"*, you know (a) that there is a 98% chance he will buy it, and (b) there is a 98% chance that you will be able to get the *exact* price you want for the car. That is why I have always regarded first class preparation as being so important. First impressions often force a snap decision and cause people to overlook and perhaps even forgive minor flaws which are almost inevitable in any vehicle.

HOW TO FLOG A LANDMARK

Should you be unfortunate enough to be stuck with a bit of a landmark, there is really only one successful way to rid yourself of the darn thing and that is to adopt the following tactics. When someone eventually rings up and remarks that he has noticed the vehicle has been advertised for some time, give him the impression that plenty of people would have bought it from the first advert but for the fact that you have been let down by a timewaster. Most people have experienced similar situations in their lives so are sympathetic to this line. As you chat to the interested party, it is then quite easy to bring the conversation round to the point where it appears that you are doing him a favour by letting him come and buy it. This way, he feels he is being given a second chance at a bargain which he would otherwise have missed, which will often push a sale through really quickly.

FIX A TIME

Last but not least, when someone rings up about a car and says he want to come and see it, always fix an *exact time.* Never stand for this *"Are you going to be around all day?"* bit. Tell him that you are in and out in the car and you must know more or less exactly when he is going to turn up, at least to within half an hour or so either way. Even better, ask him what time he aims to leave home. Once he has focused his addled brain on an exact leaving time, he has unwittingly made an appointment with you, and in doing so, is much less likely to let you down. This technique is a very good way of filtering out timewasters and I am sure that this simple precaution is the reason why I have suffered so few of them over the years.

SELLING FROM HOME

Equally as important, if you are selling a car from home, always park it within sight of the house and keep an eye on it. If potential buyers ask when they ring whether it is outside in the street, tell them it isn't, because otherwise this type of person will simply turn up early, take a butchers at the car, and then clear off without giving you the chance to put any of your sales techniques into practice. If necessary, give the impression that the vehicle is in a garage around the corner and will have to be fetched. At the end of the day, when they turn up you could always say that you have just brought it around. However, it is absolutely *essential* to prevent them from looking at the vehicle without you having the chance to make your pitch.

SYNOPSIS OF SELLING TECHNIQUE

1. Don't be pushy; appear friendly, genuine, laid back.
2. Give the impression from the start that there has been considerable response to your advert.
3. Fix an exact appointment, put him under subtle obligation by offering to hold the car for him.
4. When showing the car, always appear quietly confident. Be polite and cheerful without overdoing the charm. Casually show up the good points of the car without appearing to oversell it.
5. Hold your ground in the bidding. Always remain calm and polite, no matter how hard he may be haggling. Appear confident, as if you are certain plenty of other people will be prepared to buy it even if he doesn't.
6. Remember, it only takes one punter to buy a car. From the moment he first rings, give him your full attention.

SAFETY FIRST

All right, so that's how to sell a car, but having scruples about taking money off people is a totally different thing to having scruples about the safety of the vehicles you sell. Business is one thing, life is another. So before you get too keen on the idea of retailing cars, do bear this in mind - *it is never, under any circumstances, worth risking an accident, possibly somebody's death on your conscience, by selling an unroadworthy car.* Apart from anything else, getting a little bit of extra profit can never be worth the risk of prosecution and an almost certain criminal record.

Also, if you are selling in the trade, please bear in mind that traders have an unwritten code of honour to declare to each other any unsafe aspect of a vehicle that they are aware of.

Transgressing this code will undoubtedly result in you becoming an 'untouchable', in which case no other traders will deal with you. Traders are realistic people, they recognise the fact that bits and pieces on a car wear out. As long as these things are declared fairly and squarely, and within reason allowed for in a price, everyone is happy.

INSPECTING A CAR FOR RETAILING

If you are considering retailing a car, it needs a much more thorough inspection than the quick checkover outlined in an earlier chapter which is intended for trade buying purposes only where time, especially at auction, is often limited. If you haven't got the facilities or expertise to check a car thoroughly yourself, then either get a properly trained mechanic to do so or go to one of these 'While You Wait' franchise operations which are in every town these days specialising in safety items like tyres, brakes, steering and shock absorbers. The great thing about these places is that they will do an inspection straight away nine times out of ten, and also the checkover will be *free!* Remember, you only have to go wrong once. Major safety items, like brakes, steering, shock absorbers and tyres, are relatively inexpensive (especially when bought at trade discount) so any vehicle can be put in a safe condition without breaking the bank. *If there isn't a sufficient profit margin in the car to do that, then you shouldn't be even considering retailing it to the public in the first place.* It is particularly for these considerations that when you are starting out and can only afford to deal in bangers, you are much safer to stay within the trade, just buying and selling between garages and auction.

PART II

CHAPTER THIRTEEN

STARTING UP AS A RETAILER

Those readers who are fortunate enough to have sufficient capital resources available, or facilities for raising the necessary capital, may be considering going straight into retail motor trading and therefore may be wondering what the best way to go about it is. It is not possible to recommend any particular way as being the best as such, because there are so many variable factors connected with individual circumstances. For instance, much will depend on the kind of vehicles you intend to retail, the amount of capital you actually have available, and other factors such as geography, i.e. your location and catchment area. However, it may be helpful to you if we discuss a few basic points on the subject which will give you some food for thought.

Depending on how much capital you have to inject into the project, a first consideration is whether you are going to rent your pitch or buy it. This decision can sometimes be influenced by whether the place you have in mind enjoys residential status. In other words, if you don't mind living above the premises as well as running your business there, this may put you in a better position financially because then you may only need to take out one mortgage or bank loan. At any rate, this sort of arrangement will most certainly cut your general overheads, which can often make the difference between making a decent 'wedge' or just a living. It is also possible that banks and other lending institutions may look slightly more favourably on a business with residential status attached because they are shrewd enough to realise that a person living on the premises is likely to put in more hours. This can be a nice arrangement but remember, looking on the black side, if the business folds up for any reason, you could easily end up losing your home as well this way, which would prove pretty serious if you have a wife and family.

I have mentioned many times in this book already that retail motor trading is a capital intensive business. You do need to have considerable funds available to tie up in stock vehicles, and it is quite amazing how quickly the figures tot up. For instance, let us say that the average trade price of a clean 'retailable' car is £3,000. Well, you won't have much of a business going unless you are holding at least twenty of these, so that comes to £60,000 before you even start thinking about financing the pitch from which to the sell them! This is almost certainly the reason why most would-be retailers start off by renting forecourt space rather than buying it.

Some dealers actually start out without even renting their own pitch at all! Instead, they offer their cars to other dealers with available space on their forecourt on a 'sale or return' basis (SOR). For instance, they may have a friend with a pitch who has all his available money tied up in vehicles but, having room for a few more, is willing to carry some on a shared commission basis. This mutually beneficial arrangement is quite common in the motor trade. I know at least one highly successful motor trader who started out as a retailer by simply placing cars on other people's forecourts for the first ten years of his career. In fact, I can think of one now who has at least twenty cars at any one time sitting on various forecourts belonging to other people, a man with nerve, to be sure!

In the short term, it is worth considering approaching petrol stations locally and asking them whether they would like to enter into some form of arrangement to display a few cars. Whether they can or not may well depend on local planning laws and/or the conditions of their lease, etc, but it is surprising how many petrol stations are starting to do this. It can prove a very effective way of selling cars, because when people stop to refuel, they may notice a particular car on show and, as they are standing there filling up, they have time to think about it. The great advantage in petrol station forecourts is that potential customers have stopped anyway and are already out of their car, which is half the battle. It may sound silly, but many people are too lazy or in too much of a rush to stop and inspect a car on a normal forecourt, even if it catches their eye from the road and they are actually looking for that model! Another advantage of petrol stations is that people often feel more relaxed looking at cars this way; a shy punter doesn't always feel comfortable stopping at a garage to look at a car because he feels that a fast-talking salesman will start pressurising him, whereas in a petrol station situation, he knows he can take a butchers at the car without being hassled.

It is important to bear in mind that, if you are using other people's forecourts, it is particularly important that the cars you sell are not going to give comeback problems or the people renting you the space are soon going to want you to cease trading there and will find another dealer to take over from you.

THE IMPORTANCE OF LOCATION

Whether you are renting or buying forecourt space, you will have to give some thought to location. Obviously, you want as many people as possible to see the cars which you have up for sale. Ideally, you want a place fronting a main arterial road in or just on the outskirts of a city or town. However, always bear in mind that the more popular and well placed the position, the more you will have to pay for it and therefore the higher your overheads will become. It is worth bearing in mind that the location of your pitch is also affected by the types of vehicles which you sell. For instance, for the run-of-the-mill cars, the better placed the location, the more cars you are likely to turn over, but if you specialise in a particular field of specialist vehicles such as sportscars, classics, or perhaps even light commercials, your location becomes less important because the customers who seek these more specialist vehicles will be prepared to hunt you out. It is often the case, therefore, that specialist dealers are able to keep their overheads lower than the mainstream dealers by operating from less popular locations with lower rents and rates, perhaps on the outside of town or out on industrial estates. Indeed, if we take an extreme example to illustrate this point, the majority of really specialist traders who deal in the likes of Ferraris, are located in quite tucked away places, often in villages deep in the country. However, this does not adversely affect their trade in any way because the people who want this type of car are prepared to, and perhaps even prefer to, seek them out even if this involves some travelling.

CHOOSING YOUR STOCK

Entering the business at this level is a very different thing to starting out buying bangers from the trade or at auction. No-one can recommend exactly which models you should go for because there are too many variables in each individual case, like how much capital is available to put into stock, what sort of cars the local competition are selling, and the fact that the popularity of particular models varies so much from one area of the country to another. However, what I can do is suggest that before you start stocking your pitch, you should spend a few weeks going around as many local garages as possible and noting down which models appear to sell the fastest and their comparative prices. This should also give you an indication of what sort of cars *don't* sell well in your area, which is almost as important.

A quicker and easier way of investigating this is to carefully study your local *AutoTrader* type magazine. You will be able to assess by the frequency of adverts reappearing, how quickly certain models sell, both in the trade and also privately. This will save a lot of time running around looking at forecourts, because usually most of the successful garages in the area take out large adverts in magazines like this, displaying most or even all of what they have for sale at any one time and as they turn over stock, this will be reflected in their weekly adverts. However, having said this, I still think it is worthwhile doing some leg work around your local garages as well; it is surprising how much information you can pick up in casual conversations with your future competitors.

At the end of the day, personal preference will always play a part in the final choice of vehicles bought for stock. Unless you intend to specialise in one particular line like sports or classics, probably the best policy is to try to offer as wide a choice of popular models and types of vehicle as possible.

*For instance, don't try telling someone that a certain model
corners well when it is common knowledge that the thing handles
like a 'drunk camel on roller-skates'!*
– p. 110

CHAPTER FOURTEEN

SELLING CARS FROM
SHOWROOMS AND FORECOURTS

Assuming that you have accumulated sufficient experience and enough capital to set up as a motor dealer with premises, and retailing on a professional basis is the way you wish to proceed, then the way in which you relate to your customers and the sales techniques you will need to employ are totally different to those outlined in Chapter Twelve which are intended to effect a quick sale once in a while through the newspapers.

As I have mentioned in the previous chapter, retailing is a big subject, so we have to take certain assumptions for granted, such as that you intend to offer a wide selection of good quality models and that they will be well presented in reasonably attractive surroundings. Having accepted these factors, therefore, the only component left that is necessary to ensure the success of the retail operation is good salesmanship.

The first step to becoming a successful salesman is to have a hard think about everything you already know about what makes a *bad* salesman. Think back to all those occasions when you have not only been in car showrooms, but also into any kind of retail premises in which the salesman on hand made you feel uncomfortable, perhaps under pressure. You didn't buy anything, did you? No, exactly. Not only that, but you got out of the place as quickly as you possibly could and perhaps even avoided going there again!

People, as I have already said, are placed under stress particularly when buying cars. The analysts tell us that for the average person, the purchase of a car is the second largest capital investment they make, with their home being the first. Whether or not this is true, it is certainly the case that it is a sufficiently worrying experience for the average punter to keep a wary eye on any car salesman whilst his other half keeps a wary eye on the conjugal wad. It is vital, therefore, to relax people when they first come in to see you. If they have never met you before, they will almost certainly be on the defensive. Unfortunately, everyone harbours prejudices against car dealers, quite unfairly of course, but I am afraid you just have to accept the fact that it comes with the territory. The vast majority of people in the trade these days just want to make a decent living and the better the cars they can sell, the less hassle they get from customers, which suits everyone. However, inevitably this is an occupation against which people generally hold a negative attitude; so what you have to do in order to succeed is to turn this to your positive advantage by becoming the most popular car dealer in your area.

This sounds all very nice, you may say, but how can it be achieved? Well firstly, by following the example set by successful professionals in all fields of selling. When a really good car salesman first meets potential customers, he doesn't start straight in by trying to push any particular model at them on his pitch without finding out something about their requirements first. By taking the trouble to discuss their motoring needs with them and indeed possibly even clarifying these for them, you will not only relax them quickly but also impress them by your thoughtful and considerate attitude.

It is surprising just how many people there are out there who have only a vague idea of what they are actually looking for; anyone who leads them by the hand can only be regarded by them in a positive light. Having had a good chat with them to establish a reasonably clear idea of which models will suit them, you can, at this point, employ a well-proven sales technique used by many professionals. Instead of going ahead and recommending the appropriate models which you have in mind for them, pick out a couple of *unsuitable* cars at random which you know will definitely *not* suit them and then explain the reasons why. For instance, if they have come to look for a second car, perhaps for the wife, you can casually pass comment on a large gas guzzler on your pitch which isn't very economical and then dismiss this with an explanation of its unsuitability, moving on swiftly on to, perhaps, a 'hot hatch' with a high insurance rating as another example of an unsuitable choice. This technique has a twofold effect. Firstly, it makes you appear all the more considerate, particularly if you employ it casually in the course of discussing their general needs; and secondly, and more importantly, when you move on to show them the models which you *do* have in mind for them, your comments concerning the suitability of these will appear far more credible, and potential customers will take a great deal more notice of your expert opinion. Once they have decided that you are on their side and have their best interests at heart, they will be like putty in your hands!

THE 'RING AROUND THE TRADE' PLOY

Now here's a good tip. If having had a good discussion with your prospective customers, you decide that you do not have a vehicle in stock which is suitable for their needs, come straight out and say so and then offer to 'ring around the trade' on their behalf. They will always be extremely impressed, firstly by your honesty in not attempting to sell them an unsuitable vehicle, and secondly by the trouble you are prepared to take on their behalf.

At the end of the day, you are intending to establish a long term reputation; it is sometimes better to risk losing a sale than to sell a customer the wrong car. In fact, your honesty can only stand you in good stead because even if the particular people in question end up buying elsewhere, they will be so impressed by your attitude and helpfulness that they will make every effort to give you another chance when they change the car again. Furthermore, because they will feel somewhat guilty about not buying from you despite all your trouble, they will go out of their way to send others to your establishment by singing your praises to everyone they know who is looking for a car, and indeed, nothing about your good character will lose anything in the telling either! I know a highly successful retailer, who reckons he gains at least two sales for every one he loses by doing this.

KNOW YOUR CARS

The importance of knowing your cars well cannot be emphasised enough. Once you have taken a vehicle in, always read up on its salient technical points and its performance/economy figures so that you can make a comparison with its competition. Nothing will *unimpress* a punter more quickly than discovering he knows more about a car than you do. Believe you me, I have seen it happen to many an inexperienced car salesman and it is very embarrassing indeed. Never make the mistake of under-estimating a customer's potential knowledge concerning the technical aspects of cars. In fact, in short, never get egg on your face. Real professionals in any field know their subject inside out. Also, it is a real *faux pas* to make claims about a vehicle which are clearly untrue; if a punter knows otherwise, this will make him suspicious of your sincerity and knowledge. For instance, don't try telling someone that a certain model corners well when it is common knowledge that the thing handles like a 'drunk camel on roller skates'!

TEST DRIVING

Never underestimate the importance of a test drive. Despite what anyone says about there being no obligation and so forth, there is no doubt that a good test drive often helps to push through a sale. There are plenty of joyriders about, of course, but the sales techniques that you have employed in order to find out about people's motoring needs will also act as a useful safeguard for filtering out timewasters who are simply looking for a good day out. When taking people for test drives, try to choose a good route that you know well and stick to it. Preferably avoid heavy traffic and stressful surroundings; ideally choose the quietest, most traffic-free road you can find, especially when letting customers drive the car because it is precisely when people are driving unfamiliar vehicles, particularly ones which don't belong to them, that accidents most frequently occur! In fact, on that point, *always check that your customers are well insured first (unless your own motor trade insurance covers customers for test drives) and that they have a current driving licence.* Accidents really do happen very easily in unfamiliar cars. You know the sort of thing, some old chap fumbling with the controls trying to sort out the difference between the wipers and the indicators whilst he is reversing, so he just doesn't notice that lamp post!

STRIKING THE DEAL (THE KILL)

A good motor trader is like a white hunter, he has a highly developed killer instinct which runs deep in his psyche, he collects punters' heads to hang on his wall like the hunter does his trophies, and he hates to see one slip away!

Ultimately, there will come a point where either a deal is going to be struck or it isn't. The golden rule here is, don't be too inflexible in your profit policy. For instance, sometimes it is better to turn over a vehicle quickly and accept slightly less profit than it is to hold that vehicle for months. Treat every deal on its own merits. Part exchanges are complicated, and they do require a certain philosophical attitude because on some you will gain, and on others you will lose. The only general rule of thumb here is, be as generous as you can be, consistent with making a healthy profit, of course, on your car, because the allowance you offer a customer will be a major factor in his decision as to whether to do the deal or not.

Returning once more to the old theme of people balancing on a knife-edge of indecision, it is important to recognise that often something relatively insignificant will tip the balance and push a deal through. When a punter is standing there havering about, remember, he is probably not only weighing up your deal but comparing it to others which he has been offered recently by other dealers in the area. Your best bet at this point is to try to make an assessment of the man's character (or indeed his wife's, just as importantly, perhaps more so), and then take a guess at what little titbit you could offer which would turn a 'maybe' into a 'yes'. An obvious example is to throw in six months' road tax, but there are others like mechanical warranty insurance schemes (see *'How To Get Trade Benefits'* section) or perhaps even a fitted stereo cassette system if your profit margin on the car warrants it. Sometimes it can be as simple as a smart set of wheel trims or a tow hitch. Learning to recognise what makes the difference to any particular type of person, of course only comes with experience but this is a useful tip to bear in mind.

Retail motor trading, therefore, really comes down to understanding your fellow man in all his shapes and forms. If, through this understanding you can develop a helpful and positive approach to your customers, the benefits you will reap will be *many* in terms of reputation and success.

SYNOPSIS OF SUCCESSFUL SELLING FROM RETAIL PREMISES

1. Don't be pushy - aim to relax people as quickly as possible.

2. Take trouble to talk about their needs before discussing any of your cars.

3. Know your stuff technically - don't get caught out.

4. Lose a sale rather than sell the customer the wrong car - and gain free advertising for life.

5. Never underestimate the importance of a test drive.

6. Learn to recognise the little things that can push a deal through and when to use them to best effect.

7. Remember, it takes nearly a lifetime to establish a good reputation but only about a week to make a bad one.

PAYMENT

This is a very important topic, because at the end of all your hard work in pushing through a deal, it is necessary to extract your punter's hard earned dosh as deftly and as painlessly as possible. The four most common ways of receiving payment for a car are:

1. Cash

2. Building Society cheque

3. Banker's Draft

4. Ordinary cheque.

Taking these one at a time, firstly, in the case of cash, there are no complications. Unfortunately, when a deal involves more than a few hundred pounds, most people don't want to deal with cash, so that brings us rapidly to other methods of payment.

Secondly, in the case of a building society cheque, this is a cheque which is made out *by the building society itself* to a specific payee, in this case, your garage. It is, in fact, technically speaking, a secure method of payment because the building society actually takes the funds from a person's account before issuing a cheque which is drawn on their capital rather than the customer's. However, two words of warning concerning these. Firstly, *don't* confuse a building society cheque with a personal cheque drawn through a building society account. These days, some building societies have cheque account facilities like banks. Secondly, although a genuine building society cheque is technically secure, *it can still be stopped after it has been issued and before it has cleared through the banking system.* For instance, in an extreme case, if someone were to buy a car from you and then decide subsequently that they don't want it for some reason, they could possibly kick up enough fuss to persuade the building society to stop payment on the cheque. Admittedly, this is very unlikely; however, it still means that this method is not 100% secure.

Once upon a time, Banker's Drafts used to be regarded as the safest form of payment in existence outside of cash. *Not any more,* due to the fact that Banker's Drafts are reasonably easy for professional forgers to copy, so much so that in a recent case I read about, the major High Street bank concerned couldn't tell the difference between the forgery and one of their own Drafts.

Whenever you are offered a Banker's Draft in payment for a vehicle, it is essential to take the simple precaution of slipping away on some pretext and ringing the Bank concerned for confirmation that they have in fact issued that particular Draft. Banks are quite used to being asked for confirmation like this, particularly from the motor trade or where large capital sums are involved. The subtle way to do this is to offer to make your customers a cup of coffee and slip away to another phone extension. All right, the chance of someone passing off a dud Draft on you is statistically extremely slim. However, it is always better to be safe than sorry!

Lastly, we move on to the ordinary cheque. Normally, as you know, these take three working days to clear, although to be on the safe side, it is better to work on four. However, bear in mind that this does not count weekends, and also bear in mind that if you are clearing cheques into a building society rather than a bank, it can often take much longer, sometimes as long as ten days. The best way of clearing ordinary cheques, and indeed building society cheques, is to go for *special clearance* through your bank or building society. This can be done for a charge of approximately £10 and special clearance cheques will normally be cleared within twenty-four hours; you will be contacted by telephone to inform you whether or not the payment is securely in your account.

It is normal business practice when selling cars from established retail premises to clear cheques before allowing the customer to take delivery of the car. If you are selling from home, you should stick to this principle too. However, whereas people may be willing to do this when buying from a garage, they may often be reluctant to leave a cheque when buying vehicles from a private house which is quite understandable. This problem brings us back to cash. The main reason why most people don't want to pay in cash is because they are afraid of carrying so much and think they may be mugged. So if you have a customer who wants to buy a car from you but is reluctant to pay in cash, the problem can sometimes be resolved by offering to meet them at their bank with the car and do the transaction actually in the bank. The customer hands over the cash and you

114

hand over the registration documents and the keys for the car which is parked nearby.

THE REGISTRATION DOCUMENT TRAP

Some people believe it is safe to release a vehicle on a cheque if they hold on to the registration document until the cheque clears. This can prove to be a dangerous mistake. Today, the registration document is no longer proof of legal ownership in itself anyway, but, more importantly, if someone wants to do the dirty on you, they can simply slip you a rubber cheque and then send off to Swansea for another registration document using a V62 form which is obtainable at any Post Office. Having got this, they can simply use a new MOT Certificate in order to tax the vehicle and so forth.

It is fair to say that you cannot trust anyone these days, unless you personally know them very well, of course. Do not count on the police necessarily being interested in helping recover a car sold on a bouncing cheque because these days, unless actual forgery or other provable criminal activity is involved, they may not be. Depending very much on the individual circumstances of cases, the police often regard this sort of thing as being a matter to be settled between the two parties involved through private litigation, in which case they may very well be reluctant to become involved.

DEPOSITS

Naturally, unless the full amount is offered straight out, it is a wise move to take a small deposit. Normal business practice is to take 10% of the full value, but, of course, this can often be more than anyone has on their person at the time. In my opinion, it is better to take a relatively small deposit on the understanding that if you are let down, you keep it, rather than a larger one which you might have to give back. The law is rather unclear on the subject of deposits, but basically, there is one golden rule. When you take a deposit, make sure it is *mutually agreed in writing* that it is a real deposit, taken in good faith and *non-returnable* in the event of your customer deciding not to proceed with the deal for any reason within an agreed time period stipulated in your written agreement. Having got this down in writing, make sure that you both *sign it* and each have a copy. Remember, however, this sort of thing has to be done extremely tactfully because, if handled clumsily, it could actually put people's backs up and could possibly even lose you a deal which you have worked hard to put together.

*A good motor trader is like a white hunter, he has a highly developed
killer instinct which runs deep in his psyche, he collects punters'
heads to hang on his wall like the hunter does his trophies,
and he hates to see one slip away!*
– p. 111

CHAPTER FIFTEEN

SPECIAL INTEREST VEHICLES

When starting out in motor dealing, as I have frequently mentioned, it is safest to stick with a narrow range of bread-and-butter cars. However, at some stage, with more money to play with and the benefit of experience, you may wish to consider experimenting with other types of vehicles. Whether you are intending to become a trade dealer or retail cars, you should be aware that certain types of vehicles have some sort of image attached to them which adds to their value, inflating it beyond the sum total of their parts. I call this 'emotive value'.

This image concept does not only relate to expensive prestige vehicles like Rolls Royce, but also applies to many older cars at the cheaper end of the market, the most obvious of which are sports and classics, but it is important to realise that there are others as well, as I will explain presently.

The motor trade is divided into two camps about these sorts of vehicles. Some dealers shy away from them, regarding some of the older sports cars etc., as potential warranty nightmares (valid point, quite often); others, however, swear by them. Those that do like them maintain that the more 'emotive value' or image which a car possesses, the quicker it will sell and the more profit there is to be made out of it.

Certainly the profit potential in this type of vehicle can be high, but objectively speaking, it is wise to bear two points in mind before deciding you want to become involved in this sector of the market. Firstly, the selling and profit potential of a certain model may well depend on the area in which you live. Secondly, although the potential rewards may be greater, often so can the risk of incurring expensive repairs and problems. If you are considering retailing vehicles like these, it can often cost a great deal more to make them roadworthy and safe than ordinary everyday cars. My advice is not to rush into vehicles like these without careful thought and definitely not until you have gained experience with bread-and-butter cars first.

A punter who wants a vehicle to be not only a means of transport but also an image projector as well often displays extraordinary buying behaviour. For instance, many an otherwise quite sensible young lady will pay well over the odds for an old, clapped out Citroen Dyane or 2CV6 (usually in a horrible yellow colour and covered in 'Save the Whale' stickers!) rather than buy a Mini or Metro for less, because she feels it reflects a certain image that she wants to be identified with. For the same reason, the 'Green Welly Brigade' go overboard on Range Rovers, Discoveries and the like and many a 'Hooray Henry' is prepared to fork out a fortune to risk his neck in some old ragtop because he mistakes it for a sportscar when, for the same money, he could have bought a car that actually goes around corners (Okay ya, Nigel!).

The most notable example of this peculiar buying behaviour has to be the four-wheel drive market. Over the last ten years, car manufacturers have spent billions of Pounds, Francs, Dollars and Deutschmarks on research and development in order to make the average family car faster, smoother, safer and more economical. Despite this, and the fact that mankind is meant to be developing some global consciousness concerning the erosion of the ozone layer and his greedy overconsumption of the earth's fossil fuel supplies, what sort of vehicle does the successful-middleclass-throughout-the-whole-of-western-society aspire to? Is it a comfortable five-seater saloon packed to the brim with hi-tec, lean-burn technology and ABS braking, capable of carrying the entire family across Europe at high speed in great comfort and safety whilst running on a mere whiff of an oil rag perhaps? Not on your life! What they really want is some great slow lumbering tank of a four-wheel drive which pitches and weaves its way round corners like a tramp steamer in a high sea, whilst belching out clouds of disgusting diesel fumes, for no other reasons than fashion and status!

If you question their choice, you will be bombarded with a barrage of plausible-sounding explanations for their purchase decision, *'lots of room for the kids in the back, nice high seating position for visibility, economical for the size of vehicle, and above all else, safety'.* All this is complete cobblers, of course; if they really wanted these things, one of the new generation of surprisingly less popular 'space wagons' like the Renault Espace, could do the job faster, more smoothly and a great deal more economically. However, it doesn't enjoy the same status symbolism, it doesn't have a four-wheel drive knob on the floor, and therefore it doesn't make the grade in the golf club car park.

No, but I am afraid to say that no logical comparison with space wagons or the like will convince your average Mrs.-ex-Volvo-Estate-driver-moving-upmarket, because when hubby secures that promotion, the first thing on the shopping list is a nice, large four-wheel drive; the fact that it doesn't fit in the garage because it is about eight feet tall and that they are never going to go anywhere more muddy than the supermarket car park is completely irrelevant. That's what her sister-in-law's husband drives so that's what they're damned well going to have!

I hope you don't get the impression that I am anti four-wheel drive, nothing could be further from the truth. Actually I love them, but I do an extraordinary thing with mine, I bury it up to the axles in mud frequently and therefore, in the same spirit as I often thrash the nuts off the Ferrari, I use it as its makers intended! The point that I have been trying to make here is to get you to realise just how powerful emotive value is, and that despite all the technological advancements of recent years, when it comes to buying motors, often the punter's heart still rules over his head!

WHAT SORT OF VEHICLES HAVE EMOTIVE VALUE

1. All sportscars, from MGBs through to Ferraris.

2. All classic cars, from Morris Minors to vintage Bentleys.

3. 'Off beat' cars like Citroen Dyane or 2CV6.

4. All FWD drives, from Suzuki Jeeps through to Range Rovers.

Many a 'Hooray Henry' is prepared to fork out a fortune to risk his neck in some old ragtop because he mistakes it for a sportscar when, for the same money, he could have bought a car that actually goes around corners (Okay ya, Nigel!).
– p. 120

CHAPTER SIXTEEN

PRESTIGE AND PERFORMANCE CARS

The prestige and performance car end of the market is, in my opinion, the most interesting and, without doubt, potentially the most lucrative sector of the whole car dealing spectrum. Beware, however, it is no place for well-heeled beginners to take a shortcut to the top. The pitfalls are many and survival requires a fine understanding of the marketplace and the punters who frequent it. Only those with several years' experience of conventional motor dealing should consider entering it.

Success in this end of the market essentially depends on two things. Firstly, acquiring an understanding of the psychological attitudes of your customers, and secondly, having the nerve to ask for and get exorbitant profits. The dealers who operate in this end of the market, like the vehicles they sell, are divided into two categories. The majority of them deal in vehicles of prestigious marques, whether new or used, which are still in current production. A small percentage of dealers, however, just concentrate on the more specialist market consisting of specific models from famous marques which are not necessarily in current production any longer, but command high prices due to their collectability. For the sake of definition I shall refer to these two different types of vehicles as Category 1 and Category 2 respectively. Just to give you a basic idea of what I mean by these categories, I have drawn up a couple of short lists of a few vehicles which fall into each category.

Let's look at the dealers who trade in Category 1 vehicles first. Actually, there is not very much of interest to expand on regarding this sector of the market because, apart from being more specialist and up-market, it really operates in a similar way to any other part of the retail motor trade. The only significant difference between dealers is in the vehicles they sell; normally they specialise in one or two particular makes. Some prefer to stick with vehicles like BMW and Porsche because they feel they are intrinsically more reliable, whereas others prefer to be more adventurous and go for the Italian mob, Ferrari, Maserati and Lamborghini. There are even a few dealers who stock a cross section of models from various different manufacturers, but these tend to be ones which are not actually franchise holders for any particular marque, and therefore, generally speaking, they can only deal in used models.

Category 2 vehicles are another matter altogether. Because they are no longer in current production, their values are less well-defined and are largely governed by supply and demand and indeed all those other free market forces which we hear economists banging on about. However, if you are the right sort of person, it will be in this sector of the car market that the richest pickings are to be plucked, so let's have a closer look at the most important aspect of it, which is the customers.

THE RICH PUNTER

It is when you are dealing with these Category 2 vehicles that understanding the psychology of the people who buy this kind of car becomes so important. In this market, if you can get inside the punter's head, you are more than half way to success already. I suppose this requires a certain innate ability which is probably why so much of the mainstream motor trade misunderstands this sector of the market.

The first thing to realise is that you are dealing with punters with dosh; we are not talking about the aspiring pension plan salesman struggling to meet the monthly payments on his Porsche here, we are talking about people with serious wad. The second thing to realise is that people with enough disposable income or capital, as chartered accountants call it, to buy these cars don't really buy them to use seriously; they already have a Range Rover or a BMW to do that. No, they buy their Daytona or Miura to pose around in down at the pub on Sunday or at the race meeting. Personally I believe that all cars should be used as they were designed and intended to be used, and, luckily for me, I know a handful of fellow Ferrari enthusiasts who feel the same. But the sad fact is that for every person who actually drives a Ferrari properly, there are ten who will keep them cosseted in air-conditioned garages merely taking them out on the odd sunny Sunday or to the occasional Concourse event. The result of all this madness is that your average Category 2 buyer is only interested in very low mileage vehicles; goodness knows why, because he isn't going to add any mileage anyway, but there it is.

The result of this obsession with very low mileage leads, unfortunately, to a good deal of skulduggery. In the opinion of many enthusiasts, this end of the market suffers from more clocking on a proportionate basis than any other. So often, rare cars appear with improbably low mileages which cannot be supported by appropriate documentation. Are we to believe that, in all seriousness, a car which is over thirty years old has done less than 500 miles a year? In rare and exceptional cases, of course, this can happen, but I can honestly say, based on my experience of coming across vehicles which have ridiculously low odometer readings for their year and condition, that mileages have to be taken with a shovel-load of salt at this end of the market. Ironic really, isn't it? I mean, when you think of the fuss that is made about bread-and-butter cars being cuckoo'd, it is quite amazing that, in a market where cars can change hands for hundreds of thousands or even millions of pounds, it is almost accepted that odometer readings are as trustworthy as politicians' promises.

The third thing to realise is that because the people who buy vehicles like this do so largely for image purposes, they are so keen to obtain them that they will part with vast sums even though the cars come with little or no guarantee whatsoever. Furthermore, when something goes wrong with them, they are quite prepared to spend vast sums to put them right! This has, in itself, quite a lot to do with image as well. The people who buy these cars have always been brought up to believe that exotic vehicles are temperamental and they look upon this aspect as part of the price they have to pay in order to have the ultimate status symbol. This flies in the face of normal buying behaviour. For instance, if Henry had spent his £60,000 on a brand new Porsche rather than a 20-year old Ferrari Boxer, it would have been a very different story; he would have been knocking on the dealer's door the moment the air conditioned glove box broke down! This attitude is all the more strange when one considers that most of the people who are in a position to buy these rare cars became rich through being exceptionally shrewd and hard-headed. Yet it often appears that when it comes to buying their ultimate toys, they seem to lose their heads and go all silly. Now of course, the dealers who are doing well out of this end of the market understand this extraordinary fact very well, but the majority of the motor trade appear to be totally unaware of it. Because the average trader is used to a punter coming back screaming when the window handle falls off the 3-year old Cavalier he has just flogged him, he cannot believe that a person paying ten times as much for an old Ferrari won't do the same, which is why the majority of the motor trade doesn't want to touch stuff like this and why those who do can make a lot of money out of it.

The fourth thing to realise about this end of the market is that it is an 'all or nothing' situation. It is only the very rarest and most prestigious vehicles that make the grade. Just because people with a lot of money are prepared to go silly over old Ferraris and the like, do not for one second be lulled into assuming that people with slightly less money will act just as crazily with vehicles of less rarity. A punter who buys a Dino may be quite happy to bung in a new clutch after only a thousand miles or so, but just you see what happens if you try selling a 944 Porsche like that. Oh dear, no! After all, a 944 is a serious car, one that is actually meant to run and possesses a strong image of reliability etc. Not advisable!

VALUE FLUCTUATIONS

Right, that's enough about the punters in the market, now we come to the money. The prestige and performance market is all about nerve. If you have the nerve to go all the way and buy the most prestigious cars, you can make the most outrageous profits from them. The fact that there has been a severe downturn in the market in terms of values from the over-inflated late eighties is irrelevant; the profit margins are still there and, because the retail prices are lower, you are quite likely to turn over more cars. I know of a chap who bought a brand new 288GTO Ferrari in 1984 for around £84,000; three years later he sold it for £700,000. That car today would sell for around £200,000, such is the fluctuation in this marketplace.

As you know, during the hype period, some cars changed hands for millions of pounds. These market leaders pulled up the rest of the hyped-up market behind them and vastly inflated the value of all cars of the same or similar marques. Today, however, at the lower end of the prestige market, the cheaper Ferraris are changing hands relatively fast again, now that prices have come down to more realistic levels; there is plenty of scope in the Category 2 market to make money for those who know what they are doing and have done their research well. Cars will never be super cheap again, as in being able to buy a good Aston or Ferrari for under £10,000, but at least the market is more stable and likely to remain so for some considerable time.

PRICING VEHICLES

Well, it's all right having nerve, I hear you say, but how do you go about pricing vehicles with indefinite values like these? The answer is that when you are dealing in this market of undefined values, you have to rely a great deal on your own judgement (hence my early warning about it not being a place for rich beginners to start) based on comparing any particular car you have or are interested in, in regard to rarity, age and condition, to similar vehicles which are being advertised for sale at that time. Successful dealers in this market keep a very close eye on their competitors' cars, and constantly scan the classified columns of special interest magazines like *Classic & Sportscar* and other advertising forums such as the performance car sections of *The Sunday Times*. Actually, because *The Sunday Times* covers a fairly wide range of performance and prestige vehicles, it has almost become a price guide reference for people dealing in this market. It is worth keeping an eye on. It is also important to realise that advertising media like this can, to a certain degree, be used to manipulate the values of specific models; nothing really wrong with that, it's only playing the market forces game, but it is as well to be aware that this does sometimes go on. It was quite clearly evident back in the hype period when the prices of Ferraris would gradually rise, virtually week by week, in *The Sunday Times* and other similar publications, presumably to see how far the market could be stretched, no different to the property market, really, which is all about pushing values uphill fast in the rising cycles too.

It is important to realise, however, that value in this market is very much a subjective thing; one man's bargain £20,000 E-Type may be another man's overpriced rusting old 'dog'. It is, however, in this vague, grey area of *perceived value* that the big profit making potential lies.

PERCEIVED VALUE

The real key to making the most of perceived value is to price cars to people's level of expectation. Let me attempt to explain. Enter our pretend punter, *Mr. Fastbuck*. Right, well, *Mr Fastbuck*, having made himself an overnight fortune out of latex rubber in the commodities market due to an unprecedented surge in demand, has convinced himself he wants to buy a Ferrari 328. He does a little bit of research into prices, and scans *The Sunday Times* and motor magazines. He notices quite a discrepancy in prices between the cars advertised, he finds several of them on offer in the £35,000-£40,000 price bracket with the occasional one advertised (always as 'probably the best available') for around £45,000.

He is a shrewd man who, although rich, does not want to spend more money than necessary; however, he feels he would rather shell out a bit more and get a decent car than pay less and end up with a bit of a tart. So, as money is no problem, he mentally fixes a ceiling of £45,000. He perceives that at this price he will get one of the best cars available. Like most people in his position, he is too busy to go around and compare the actual cars themselves, and, as he is used to basing judgements on 'paper values' all day in the commodities market, he is happy to leave it at that.

Right, so let's suppose you have bought in a pretty reasonable 328 for around £32,000. You spend a little bit of time and a couple of grand toshing it up so it really looks like a 'minter'. Now it stands you in at £34,000 but it really looks the part. If you put it up for sale at £39,950, a £40,000 punter will come along and buy it quick enough to be sure. However, our rich friend, *Mr. Fastbuck*, won't bother to even give you a telephone call because he is only looking for a £45,000 car. So you *don't* put it up for £39,950, you test the market a bit further by putting it up for £42,950 and *Mr. Fastbuck* soon snaps up what he perceives as a top-of-the-range car for two grand under the going rate. He is very happy and you are even happier. That is perceived value!

MONEY

Whatever you sell your car for, the really nice thing about the top end of the market is that everyone has the cash; people don't buy this sort of car on the drip, they either have the dosh or they don't, and quite often, cash is exactly what they *do* have and want to get rid of for various reasons not entirely unconnected with a tendency towards sporadic bouts of amnesia when filling in Income Tax Returns. I shall never forget one particular, very dashing lady who turned up at my place one day with her minder (in a *pink* 911 Turbo - *urrgh!*) covered in pearls and diamonds; in fact she had so many diamond rings on that every time she stroked the lines of the Ferrari she was looking at, she was in danger of scratching the paintwork down to the undercoat. *"It's my birthday,"* she chirped brightly, *"and my husband said I could have anything I liked so I told him I wanted a Ferrari!"* After a brief test run, she opened her large handbag and tipped out a mountain of twenty pound notes, driving off leaving me several grand better off. Well, it's the redistribution of wealth, isn't it, comrade!

EXAMPLES OF THE TWO CATEGORIES

Category 1

The sort of cars that fall into this category are the *current* models of any prestigious marque. Here are a few examples.

Aston Martin

Rolls Royce

Ferrari

Maserati

Lamborghini

Lotus

Porsche

BMW

Mercedes

Category 2

The sort of cars that fall into this category are certain *specific* models which are no longer in production but which have collectable status like:

Ferrari	Daytona GTB 4/Spyder
	Dino 246/Spyder
	288 GTO
Lamborghini	Miura SV
Maserati	Bora
	Ghibli Spyder
	Merak SS
Aston Martin	DB4 GT Zagato
	DB 5/6 Volante
AC	Cobra 427/302
Porsche	911 Carrera RS 2.7 (1972-3)
Jaguar	3.8 S1/2 'E' Type Roadster

Quite often, cash is exactly what they do have and want to get rid of for various reasons not entirely unconnected with a tendency towards sporadic bouts of amnesia when filling in Income Tax Returns.
– p. 129

CHAPTER SEVENTEEN

How To Get Trade Benefits

Important - all company names and addresses quoted in this book have been placed into this section purely for the purpose of helping the reader. This does not imply that any company mentioned is particularly recommended or otherwise by the author or publishers.

TRADE INSURANCE

This is obviously the most important thing to get sorted out first. *Whatever else you do, never ever drive a car without at least third party cover.* A normal private insurance policy usually requires you to inform the company every time you change or drive another car, but this would be totally impractical for a motor trader who is picking up and delivering cars all day long. Therefore, there are special motor traders' policies available which provide 'blanket' cover for almost any vehicle that the trader has a licence to drive. These policies vary in detail; for instance, some policies exclude high performance cars, whereas others offer cover, completely irrespective of insurance grouping. It is suggested, therefore, that you compare the policies of different companies carefully to ensure that you end up with a policy which best suits your particular motor trading activities.

A word of caution, as with any insurance matter, do make sure that you end up with a reputable company which will actually pay up in the event of a claim. If in doubt, obtain some advice through one of the larger reputable insurance brokers, some of whom may be able to offer you motor trading policies from various companies. However, as it is a fairly specialist area, there are not that many companies in this particular field.

Here are some addresses of firms that advertise motor trade insurance:

Norton Insurance Brokers

Regency House
97-107 Hagley Road
Edgbaston
Birmingham B16 8LA
Tel. No. (0121) 246 5050
Will offer cover for those who trade from home, must be 23 years or older. (Additional driver over 19.)

Road Runner Limited

854 Brighton Road
Purley
Surrey CR8 2BH
Tel. No. (08707) 878 730
Will offer cover for those who trade from home, must be 25 years or older, named drivers 21 years.

Tradex Insurance

199 Ilford Lane
Ilford
Essex IG1 2RX
Tel. No. (0208) 478 6821
Will offer cover for trading from home.

Unicom Insurance

197-205 High Street
Ponders End
Enfield
Middlesex EN3 4DZ
Tel. No. (0208) 805 7799

Will offer cover for those who trade from home - fully comp cover for under 25s if driving licence held for 3 years, however, excess increases.

PRICE GUIDES

The two main Price Guides in the motor trade are, of course, 'Glass's Guide' and 'CAP Black Book'. The annual subscription for Glass's Guide is £268 for twelve monthly issues, and the CAP subscription is also £240. Obviously, neither Guide company like to supply their guides to anyone outside of the bona fide motor trade; therefore, in order to subscribe, firstly you need to ring and obtain a subscription application form, and secondly, you need to send in a copy of your letter heading or similar stationery such as a compliment slip with your trading details on it, preferably also with a photocopy of your motor trade insurance. Of course, it has to be said that, traditionally, many motor traders have started out in the business by buying *one month old* copies from a friend who is a subscriber at a reduced price, taking the viewpoint that the price of any individual vehicle, whether bought at auction or through the trade, will usually vary by more than one month's difference anyway. Although this is fairly common practice, many of these people do not realise that if the publishers of these Guides discover any subscriber selling out-of-date books like this, they may well stop supplying him.

Here are the Head Office addresses of both Glass's and CAP:

Glass's Guide Service Ltd
1 Princes Road
Weybridge
Surrey KT13 9TU
Tel. No. (01932) 823823
Annual Subscriptions:
Cars; £268 Older Cars; £150 Commercial; £228

CAP Price Guides
CAP House
Carleton Road
Skipton
North Yorkshire BD23 2BE
Tel. No. (0870) 1222211
Annual Subscriptions; Cars £240 Commercial £240

DISCOUNTS

These can sometimes be obtained by merely producing a motor trader's business card or stationery with headed notepaper but increasingly these days, parts suppliers are enforcing company rules that discounts can only be given on production of *a trade order*, that is an official order form with a business address at the top made out for whatever parts are required. Therefore, once you have gone into business as a motor trader, it is a good idea to have some of these forms printed up for you. You could do this at your local print shop, but probably it is better to do it through a company which specialises in producing motor trading stationery.

Here is the address of one of the largest and longest established motor trading stationery producers:

NEBS Standard Forms
Sovereign Way
Chester West Park
Chester
CH1 4QU
Tel. No. (0800) 304030

Overleaf are two examples of forms which are available from NEBS Standard Forms Limited for motor trading purposes.

An alternative supplier of Motortrade Stationery is:-

Romsey Business Forms
Unit 12
Budds Lane
Romsey
Hampshire SO51 0HA
Tel. No. (01794) 517206

FOUR WHEELS TO A FORTUNE

EXAMPLE OF A USED CAR APPRAISAL FORM

STANDARD FORMS

Form Ref: M302

Re-Order From: Standard Forms ..td
Tel: 0800 30 40 30
Fax: 0800 41 40 41

USED CAR APPRAISAL FORM

NAME

ADDRESS

POSTCODE

TEL: (HOME)   (WORK)

VEHICLE DETAILS

MAKE	COLOUR	ABS BRAKING	ALARM
MODEL	TRIM	AIRBAG	ROAD FUND LICENSE
REG No.	MANUAL/AUTOMATIC	RADIO/CASSETTE	MOT
CC	PETROL/DIESEL	SUNROOF	EXTRAS
VIN/CHASSIS No.	CENTRAL LOCKING	SEATBELTS	
YEAR OF MANUFACTURE	ELECTRIC WINDOWS	LEATHER	
MILEAGE	POWER STEERING	ALLOY WHEELS	

CONDITION OF VEHICLE

OVERALL CONDITION
Excel Good Avg Poor

ENGINE CONDITION
Excel Good Avg Poor

BODYWORK DESCRIPTION

ENGINE DESCRIPTION

+ SCRATCH   X DENT   (X) EXTENSIVE DAMAGE

ITEM	EXCELLENT	GOOD	AVERAGE	POOR	COMMENTS/REPAIRS/REPLACEMENT REQUIRED	PARTS COST
PAINTWORK						
PANELWORK						
UPHOLSTERY						
CARPETS						
HEADLINING						
ENGINE						
CLUTCH						
AXLES						
GEARBOX						
BRAKES						
FRONT DRIVE						
REAR DRIVE						
STEERING						
SUSPENSION						
BATTERY						
ELECTRICS						
EXHAUST						
TYRES						
CORROSION						
LABOUR						

REGISTRATION DOCUMENT INSPECTED Yes No	No. OF HOURS @ £	TOTAL LABOUR
SERVICE RECORD Complete Part None	TRADE RETAIL	TOTAL RECONDITIONING COST
ROAD TEST Good Average Poor	BUYING IN PART EXCHANGE	TRADE VALUE
SALESMAN		
	DATE OF APPRAISAL	ALLOWANCE PRICE

© Standard Forms Ltd. Tel: 0800 30 40 30 Form Ref: M302

137

FOUR WHEELS TO A FORTUNE

EXAMPLE OF A USED CAR SALES INVOICE

STANDARD
FORMS

Form Ref M15

Re-Order From: Standard Forms Ltd
Tel: 0800 30 40 30
Fax: 0800 41 40 41

USED CAR SALE INVOICE

SOLD TO		MAKE	REGISTRATION	STOCK No.
		MODEL	FIRST UK REG.	DATE OF SALE
USER where Sold to Finance Company		CHASSIS No.	ENGINE No.	MILEOMETER

SELLERS DECLARATION

Input Tax deduction has not been and will not be claimed by me in respect of the vehicle sold on this invoice.

Signature .... Date ....

SALE PRICE		
ROAD FUND LICENCE .... MONTHS		
GROSS INVOICE VALUE		
LESS PART EXCHANGE ALLOWANCE	REGISTRATION No.	
	STOCK No.	
SUB TOTAL		
LESS DEPOSIT PAID ..../ ..../		
NET AMOUNT DUE	**£**	

BUYERS DECLARATION

I certify that I am the buyer of the car sold on this invoice, at the price stated.
I UNDERSTAND THAT NO WARRANTY AS TO THE ACCURACY OF THE MILEAGE HAS BEEN GIVEN OR IMPLIED

Signature .... Date ....

FOR V.A.T PURPOSES THESE TWO INVOICES ARE ONE DOCUMENT AND SHOULD NOT BE SEPARATED

NOTE: ALL COPIES SHOULD BE SIGNED INDIVIDUALLY

PURCHASED FROM		MAKE	REGISTRATION	STOCK No.
		MODEL	FIRST UK REG.	DATE OF SALE
V.A.T. No. (if any):		CHASSIS No.	ENGINE No.	MILEOMETER

SELLER'S DECLARATION

I CERTIFY THAT:
I am the seller of the car described at the price stated.
My address is as shown above.
The mileometer reading is CORRECT/INCORRECT*
The approximate true mileage is ....
The car is free from any lien or encumbrance other than as shown on this document.
A current MOT Test Certificate HAS/HAS NOT* been handed over by me.
The Registration Document HAS/HAS NOT* been handed over by me.
The car HAS/HAS NOT* been used as a hire Car or Taxi.
The car WAS/WAS NOT* used prior to U.K. Registration.
The car HAS/HAS NOT* been the subject of a total loss claim.

Signature .... Date ....

PURCHASE PRICE		
LESS SETTLEMENT TO:		
NET INVOICE VALUE	**£**	

*THIS INVOICE HAS BEEN SETTLED BY CASH/CHEQUE
*THIS INVOICE HAS BEEN OFFSET AGAINST THE PRICE OF THE FOLLOWING VEHICLE.
REG. No.:   STOCK No.:
*Delete as applicable

© Standard Forms Ltd Tel: 0800 30 40 30 Form Ref. M15

MECHANICAL WARRANTY INSURANCE

If you thinking of retailing cars, it is an excellent idea to investigate the possibilities of getting hold of mechanical warranty insurance. This means that, providing a car meets with certain criteria in terms of age and mileage, you can offer it 'with warranty' either as an optional extra, or, if you feel so inclined and it helps to push a deal through, you can to throw it in with the price. It certainly helps to sell cars if you can offer them with a warranty available. Should something go wrong with a car which you have sold within the fixed warranty period, depending on the warranty company involved, you will not necessarily have to fix the car yourself, you can have it fixed elsewhere and the warranty company will pay whatever their agreed liability level is in that particular scheme; this can actually be the total cost involved. The best part about these schemes is that you do not have to pay a premium every year to have this insurance. You really only pay for it when you need it. Many dealers actually make a profit out of selling the warranty on to the customer; for instance, they might buy a certain level of warranty cover for about £120 and sell it on to the customer for perhaps around £220.

Here is the address of a company which can supply the trade with various types of mechanical warranty schemes:

Car Care Plan Ltd.
Bramley House
Bramley District Centre
Leeds LS13 2EJ
Tel. No. (0113) 2180000

Like this company, most warranty suppliers can offer you a range of policies to best suit the vehicles you deal in.

GETTING YOUR OWN HP FACILITIES

If you are retailing, sooner or later you will have to consider getting connected to at least one finance company. Normally, this costs you nothing, quite the opposite in fact. Every car you sell on an HP Agreement will normally earn you a little bit of commission from the HP company who, having cleared the customer for credit, will usually pay you cash up front.

There are quite a few companies specialising in the motor trade business and, providing that you are a bona fide motor dealer, there is keen competition between them to get your trade.

Here are a couple of addresses:

First National Wagon Finance
No. 3 Princess Way
Redhill
Surrey RH1 1UR
Head Office Tel. No. (0870) 6008500

Welcome Financial Services Ltd
2nd Floor
42-46 Upper Parliament Street
Nottingham NG1 2AG
Tel. No. (01159) 509444

HIRE PURCHASE PROTECTION

On the other side of the HP coin, one of the greatest dangers about buying cars from the public, or from the trade even, is the possibility that the vehicle will prove to be legally still in the possession of a hire purchase or leasing company. Approximately 70% of vehicles which are purchased new are subject to some kind of finance agreement. When you buy cars from auction, you should usually be covered by the Auctioneers' Indemnity Scheme for this eventuality; incidentally, though, always check the rules which apply to any particular auction you are attending before bidding.

Buying from the public or even from the trade without checking whether a vehicle is subject to a Lease or HP Agreement could mean a total loss of several thousand pounds. Therefore, as soon as you start expanding into the more expensive vehicles, you should consider enrolling with a company that specialises in offering protection from buying cars which are still on HP. As a subscriber, you can then ring them up before you buy a car and they will be able to tell you three things:

1. Whether there is any outstanding hire purchase or lease agreement on the vehicle recorded in their databank.

2. Whether it is on the police stolen list.

3. They will also tell you whether the car has ever been officially recorded as an insurance company write-off.

The address of HP Information is:

HPI Ltd
Dolphin House
P.O. Box 61, New Street
Salisbury, Wilts SP1 2TB
Tel: (01722) 413434
Costs - £100 joining fee plus £50 cash balance towards enquiry credits plus VAT.

Each enquiry costs £3.45 Classic Check, £4.45 Gold Check (up to £10,000) plus VAT.

Annual subscription for subsequent years £35 plus VAT.

HOW TO GET TRADE PLATES

Trade plates are special number plates which are transferable from one vehicle to another in order to be able to drive untaxed cars on the road for the purposes of moving them between auctions and premises, and demonstrating vehicles for sale if they are untaxed.

The procedure for obtaining trade plates is relatively straightforward but they are not issued automatically and may, indeed, not be granted at all. Part of the process involves the inspection of your motor trading premises by a police officer to ascertain whether your activities comply with certain conditions deemed to be essential for the granting of trade plates. In the first instance, if you are interested in applying for them, go to your local Vehicle Licensing Authority and ask for Form VTL301 called 'Application for a Trade Licence'. Please be aware that there is a certain element of discretion involved in the granting of trade plates which does tend to vary from one area to another and therefore it is difficult to be specific about exactly what the authorities in your particular area will require; the more background research you can do through local motor traders whom you know, the better it will be when you put in your own application.

MOTOR TRADE ASSOCIATION ADDRESSES

If you become an established motor trader, you may wish to join one of the following organisations. Amongst other things, they offer a conciliation and arbitration service for both motor dealers and customers with problems.

Retail Motor Industry Federation Ltd
201 Great Portland Street
London W1W 5AB
Tel: (0207) 580 9122

Scottish Motor Trade Association
3 Palmerstone Place
Edinburgh EH12 5AF
Tel: (0131) 225 3643

Vehicle Builders and Repairers Association Ltd.
Belmont House
102 Finkle Lane
Gildersome
Leeds LS27 7TW
Tel: (01132) 538333

Society of Motor Manufacturers & Traders
Forbes House
Halkin Street
London SW1X 7DS
Tel: (0207) 235 7000

Part of the process involves the inspection of your motor trading premises by a police officer to ascertain whether your activities comply with certain conditions deemed to be essential for the granting of trade plates.
– p. 141

CHAPTER EIGHTEEN

THE GOVERNMENT'S CUT!

VAT AND USED CARS

Here are a few basic points on the subject of VAT as it relates to used car dealing. I am not an expert on the subject and, whilst I have endeavoured to obtain accurate information, I must urge you *not* to regard anything stated in this section as official. The rules and regulations concerning VAT are complex and vary with individual circumstances.

The best advice anyone can give is to seek expert help from a qualified accountant at a very early stage if you think you are going to register for VAT because, if you do *not* comply with the legal requirements, you may incur severe penalties.

1. You are obliged by law to register for VAT if at the end of any month your turnover for the previous twelve months exceeds £54,000. Notification must be made to the VAT Office within thirty days of the end of the month in which the turnover limit has been exceeded.

2. If you expect to exceed an annual turnover of £54,000 in the next thirty days, you are legally obliged to register for VAT. Notification must be made to the VAT Office within that thirty day period using form 1 which is available from your local VAT office.

3. You can find your local VAT Office in the phone book under `Customs & Excise'.

4. Should you wish to register for VAT voluntarily, even if your turnover is *less* than the required amount (so that you can

claim VAT back on spare parts, petrol etc.) you can apply to do so at your local VAT Office.

5. There are special accounting procedures for used car dealers who have to account for VAT on the *gross* profit margin on ordinary cars, i.e. this margin must *include* VAT. Note, not on the *whole* price of the car and not on the *net* profit, so you *don't* deduct expenses incurred in doing up the car first because that would make the profit margin *net*. However, when you register for VAT, you can claim back VAT on things like spare parts, bodywork, and petrol used in the course of business etc.

6. In the case of commercial vehicles (or any vehicles including cars where VAT has been claimed on the whole purchase price), VAT is due on the *whole* sale price, not just the gross profit margin.

7. If you sell a car for less than you paid for it (i.e. make a loss), no VAT will be due on it, but you can't set this loss against the profits made on other cars in relation to VAT margins.

8. If you are registered, you must account for VAT on any charges made for your own services to other people and issue VAT invoices for them.

9. At the moment, you have to keep records and submit them on a quarterly basis. You will need to keep a special stock book to do this and obtain and issue proper printed invoices from suppliers and customers (see 'How To Get Trade Benefits' chapter - Standard Forms Ltd. etc.).

   If your annual turnover is under £600,000, and you have been VAT registered for twelve months, you also have the option to apply to submit your VAT returns on an annual basis but definitely seek the advice of a qualified accountant before deciding to take this option.

10. If you are setting up as a motor trader, you will be able to register for VAT early as an *intending trader* which allows you to claim VAT *before* you start selling cars and it becomes obligatory to register.

11. When you register for VAT, you can claim back VAT on equipment, up to a maximum of three years after you purchased it (providing you have kept the VAT Invoices, of course) which it to be used in your business, i.e. tools, hoists etc.

    Also, you can claim on the cost of services incurred in setting up your business (like legal fees, etc.) as far back as six months before the date you were obliged to register.

12. You can obtain a free booklet from your local VAT Office which outlines the requirements of VAT in regard to used car dealing; it is called *Public Notice No. 711 - Second Hand Cars.*

Please note that this edition of 'Four Wheels To A Fortune' was printed in March 2001 and the information contained here relates to the March 7th 2001 budget. The Regulations governing VAT may change considerably, particularly with regard to turnover level, in each subsequent budget. Always check current Regulations at your local VAT Office.

INCOME TAX

When you become a motor trader, you should register as self-employed with the Inland Revenue because there is a fine for failing to notify the Inland Revenue within six months of the end of the tax year. If you are intending to incorporate a limited company, you will become a director and may need to administer PAYE to yourself as an employee of that company.

Under the self assessment rules the basis for assessment for a self-employed person are as follows:

1. The first year's assessment is based on the profits from the commencement date to the 5th April following that commencement date.

2. The second year is based on the twelve months up to the accounting date ending in the second year of assessment.

3. The third and subsequent years are based on the accounting year ending in the year of assessment - known as 'the current year basis'. In most cases, applying the above rules gives rise to a small element of double taxing profits in the first and second years, but relief is given for this on the cessation of the business or a change of year end. This is known as overlap relief.

You will need to do some simple book-keeping (unless you have to register for VAT, then it is not quite so simple) and keep all your receipts, both for everything you buy and for the cars you sell. You don't *have* to employ an accountant to make your Tax Returns, but it is extremely advisable to do so. Apart from anything else, he should be able to recover the cost of his charges many times over through providing you with up-to-date advice on clawing back tax relief on the costs of various capital items which you can set against tax and, indeed, tax deductible expenses in general.

If you are in full time employment and on P.A.Y.E., you can still run a part-time business on Schedule D with all the advantages this can bring you.

SELF-EMPLOYED NATIONAL INSURANCE CONTRIBUTIONS

The self-employed pay National Insurance Contributions towards their State Pension and other Social Security benefits, as do 'employees'. This subject is too complex to go into in great detail over because there are a number of variable factors relating to individual circumstances which determine what contributions a particular individual makes. However, I will just try to outline the main structure of the system to give a rough guide as to how it works. Many people may not realise, for instance, that the self-employed have to pay their contributions on two levels.

CLASS 2 CONTRIBUTIONS

These are weekly contributions which must be paid either by monthly or quarterly payments, usually by Direct Debit. This is a flat rate which varies from time to time but at the moment is £2.00 a week. You cannot claim tax relief on these payments. I *think* that if you do miss paying them for a while (perhaps because money is tight in the early stages) they will allow you to back pay them up to a maximum of six years backdating. It is important that these contributions are paid otherwise your pension could be severely affected. If you earn less that a certain amount, presently around £3,995 per year, you can apply to the DSS for exemption from paying at all. The Class 2 side of the business is handled by your local DSS Office and you should contact them for details. You will discover that these contributions entitle you to most Social Security benefits but not unemployment and a few other benefits, so be sure to ask exactly what you are entitled to.

CLASS 4 CONTRIBUTIONS

Class 4 contributions are charged by the Inland Revenue if your annual taxable profits exceed a certain minimum figure. Should you be liable for these, you will pay them with your Income Tax bill.

Presumably these figures will vary from year to year, but here is a guide to give you some idea of how it works at the moment.

If your annual taxable profit is over £4,535, Class 4 contributions will be charged on this at a rate of 7% (up to a maximum of £1,775.55 if your profit is £29,900 or over).

So, all in all, very straight forward really, er.... Yes, Minister!

CHAPTER NINETEEN

TIPS AND KIT

IT WON'T START!

1. If the engine will only turn over slowly, first of all check the battery connections, particularly the positive one. Even if it looks clean, give it a quick wipe with emery paper before reconnecting. If the problem still persists, check leads to starter motor for a loose connection. If there is still no joy, test the battery and/or recharge it.

2. If there isn't a healthy spark, try pulling off the distributor cap and checking the spark at the points. If there are two of you, get the other to turn the engine over while you watch; if you are on your own, leave the ignition on and separate the points with the end of a biro to check for a flash *(holding the plastic bit to avoid a shock!)*. If there is no flash, switch off the ignition and clean the points with a piece of emery paper, then check all the connections to the distributor. If there is still no joy, suspect a duff coil or condenser. If there is a spark at the points but not at the plug lead end, try spraying the inside of the distributor cap and plug leads with WD40. Then wipe the distributor cap inside with a cloth. In the case of electronic ignition systems, as most of these are sealed units, it is only really possible to check whether there is a spark at the plugs.

3. If there is a healthy spark at the plugs, you should then suspect a fuel problem. First, unless you know there is petrol in the car, don't trust the fuel gauge. Remove the tank cap and listen for sloshing noises when you rock the car.

4. If there is petrol in the tank, check next to see if it is reaching the carburettor or fuel injector system. Sometimes, you can get a good idea of this by simply removing the top of the air filter and seeing whether the inlet track is damp with petrol vapour. If the car has a carburettor, check for a sticking carb slide which can sometimes be freed with WD40. In the case of fuel injection, if it is electronic, look for electrical connection failure first. In the case of mechanical fuel injection, check whether the drive belt is broken or slipping.

5. Incidentally, in my experience jump-starting cars should be avoided whenever possible because it does seem to have an adverse effect on the alternator of the 'donor car', sometimes drastically shortening its life. The recovery services like the AA, etc., normally equip their vans with super heavy-duty alternators which has to be more than a coincidence!

USEFUL TIPS

1. If a car is reluctant to start on a hot day, press the accelerator pedal gently to the floor and spin the engine while holding it there. This often does the trick.

2. Whenever starting a car with a weak battery, always press the clutch pedal to the floor - this relieves the starter motor of the weight of the transmission and makes the engine spin much more freely. It is always a good idea to do this when starting any car in cold weather anyway.

3. Should a car start backfiring, always suspect a duff condenser first if the vehicle has points. A cheap part to replace, but, of course, you don't always have one when you need one! A good get-you-home trick is to spray WD40 into the end of the condenser just where the wire goes into it; this will often cure the problem temporarily.

4. A car which is difficult to start will sometimes go if you pull the suppressor caps off the spark plugs and then rest them back on the end of the plugs gently; this creates a much more

powerful spark and, once the engine has cleared itself, you can *stop the engine again* (otherwise you will get a nasty shock!) and push them on properly.

5. If the starter motor jams, you can often clear it by sticking the car in gear and rocking it gently backwards and forwards with the engine off.

6. Leaking radiators can be temporarily repaired sometimes by breaking an egg and pouring the white (minus yolk) into the water if no radiator sealant is available.

7. Emergency fan belts can be made up of other things than ladies' stockings, a strong bit of cord will usually do the trick as well.

8. If a slipping clutch is due to oil leaking through from a crankshaft seal (usually detectable by oil dripping from the bottom of the clutch bell housing), it is sometimes possible to get home by pouring a fizzy drink like a cola onto the clutch through the top of the bell housing if there is an access or inspection hole. If this is done every few miles, it will usually allow the clutch to hold enough to get you home. If there are two of you, this is best done with the clutch pedal pressed to the floor. This is an old rally drivers' 'get you home' bodge.

ESSENTIAL CAR DEALER'S EQUIPMENT

If you are travelling around the auction circuit or far afield to obtain cars, then the following equipment is essential. It may look like a lot to carry, but actually if you get the right type of gear, it is very compact and, believe me, when you need any of it, you will be very grateful that you are carrying it.

1. Small can of WD40 or equivalent

2. Emergency fan belt

3. 6-inch adjustable spanner

4. Medium-sized reversible screwdriver, Phillips one end, blade the other

5. Small pair of pliers

6. Compact tow rope (the best are the flat, nylon type which fold down to fit easily in your pocket)

7. Can of tyre inflator like Tyreweld (often auction cars don't have jacks - remember *this stuff does not make a permanent repair* but it can get you to the nearest garage if you drive slowly)

8. Small powerful torch

9. Compact plug spanner

10. Small plug cleaning brush

11. Emery file for cleaning points

12. Small can of radiator sealant

13. Hose repair kit

14. Pair of jump leads

15. Useful length of HT lead suitable for either emergency replacement of coil or plug leads

16. Small roll of strong string

17. Small stash of coins for the phone or a phonecard.

Emergency fan belts can be made up of other things than ladies'
stockings, a strong bit of cord will usually do the trick as well.
– p. 153

CHAPTER TWENTY

FOUR WHEELS
TO A
FORTUNE

UK AUCTION GUIDE

AUCTION INDEX

Please Note: Auctions sometimes change the times and days of sales. It is always advisable to ring and check with any particular auction before setting off to attend it and also to obtain directions.

LONDON

Stonehill Park Auctions
Lea Valley Trading Estate
Edmonton
North London N18 3LD
Tel: (0208) 807 2300
Mon, Wed & Fri 7.00 pm

Bow Car Auctions
120 Bow Common Lane
Bow
London E3 4BH
Tel: (0207) 538 3812
Mon & Wed 7.00 pm
Fri 11.00 am

Whitechapel Car & Commercial Auctions
main entrance Fulbourne Street
London E1 5AA (other entrance
Valance Road Whitechapel
London)
Tel: (0207) 377 1422
Tue & Thur 6.30 pm
Sat 12.00 noon

LONDON contd.

Thameside Motor Auctions
Wandsworth Bridge Road
Fulham
London SW6 7TY
Tel: (0171) 736 0086
Tue & Fri 7.30 pm
Sat 1.00 pm

General Auctions Ltd
63/65 Garret Lane
Wandsworth
London SW18 4AD
Tel: (0208) 874 2955
(0208) 870 3909
Mon 2.00 pm

LONDON contd.

Wimbledon
Manheim Car Auctions
Waterside Way
Plough Lane
Wimbledon
SW17 7AB
Tel: (0208) 944 2000
Fax-U-Back: (01336) 416079)
Cars: Mon, Wed & Fri 10.30 am
Select Car Sale: Mon, Wed & Fri
10.30 am
(For specialist sales ring for details)

MIDDLESEX

Enfield
British Car Auctions
620-640 Great Cambridge Road
Enfield
Middlesex
EN1 3RL
Tel: (0208) 366 1144
Cars: Tue/Thur 11.00 am
Sat 9.30 am
Light Commercials: Tues 10.00 am
(For specialist sales ring for details)

ESSEX

Chelmsford
Chelmsford Car Auctions
Drovers Way
Chelmsford
CM2 5PP
Tel: (01245) 450700
Mon 6.30 pm - Cars
Mon 11.00 am - Vans
Wed & Sat 11.00 am - Fleet/Private,
Older Cars

Frating, Nr. Colchester
Manheim Car Auctions
Frating
Nr Colchester
Essex CO7 7DX
Tel: (01206) 250230
Tue & Thur 10.30 am - Fleet Vehicles
Thur 6.00 pm - Cars (K reg and older)
Tue & Thur 10.30 am - Trade Sales
Wed 10.00 am - Light Commercials
Every three weeks 10.00 am - Heavy
Commercials
(ring for details of other sales)

SURREY

Guildford
Guildford Car Auctions Ltd
Slyfield Industrial Estate
Moorfield Road
Guildford
Surrey GU1 1RL
Tel: (01483) 563388/571900
Mon 6.30 pm
Thur 7.00 pm
Sat 12.00 noon

Croydon
Dingwall Motor Auctions
Sidney House
Beddington Farm Road
Croydon
Surrey CR0 4XB
Tel: (0208) 684 0138
Mon & Wed 6.00 pm - Cars only
Fri 5.00 pm - Commercial
*   6.00 pm Cars*

Blackbushe
British Car Auctions
Auction Centre
Blackbushe Airport
Blackwater
Camberley
Surrey GU17 9LG
Tel: (01252) 878555
Cars: Mon 11.00 am, Wed & Fri
*   10.00 am*
Top Car Auctions: 1st & 3rd Mon
*   every month 11.00 am*
Light Commercials: Fri 10.00 am
Late Year, Low Mileage:
*   Wed 11.00 am*

KENT

Ashford
Hobbs Parker Auctions
Romney House
Ashford Market
Monument Way
Orbital Park
Ashford
Kent TN24 0HB
Tel: (01233) 502222
Mon & Wed 6.00 pm - (all vehicles)

Erith
Erith General Motor Auction
188 Manor Road
Erith
Kent
Tel: (01322) 350567
Phone for details of sales times

KENT contd.

Paddock Wood
- near Tonbridge
British Car Auctions
Eldon Way
Paddock Wood
Nr Tonbridge
Kent TN12 6BE
Tel: (01892) 836611
Cars: Tue & Fri 10.00 am
Light Commercials: Thur 11.00 am
Late Year, Low Mileage: Tue
11.00 am
Economy Line Sale: Thur 11.00 am
Distributor; Part Exchange Vehicles:
Fri 1.00 pm
Fleet Sale: Tues 10.00 am &
Fri 2.00 pm
(For specialist sales ring for details)

SUSSEX

Crawley
Crawley Car Auctions
Stephenson Way
Crawley
West Sussex RH10 1TN
Tel: (01293) 514514
Tue & Thur 6.30 pm

Eastbourne
Eastbourne Car Auctions Ltd
Auction House
Arkwright Road
Lottbridge Drove Trading Estate
Eastbourne BN23 6QL
Tel: (01323) 520295
Wed 1.00 pm
Fri 6.00 pm

SUSSEX contd.

Shoreham
Shoreham Vehicles Auctions
Chartwell Road
Lancing Business Park
Lancing
West Sussex BN15 8UB
Tel: (01903) 851200
Cars: Mon 7.00 pm &
Thur 12.00 noon
Commercial: Every two weeks 11.00 am
Commercial, Plant and Agricultural
Machinery Sales are held every
two months
(ring for details of times)

HAMPSHIRE

Southampton
Southampton Vehicle Auctions
Southern Road
Southampton
Hants SO15 1DH
Tel: (02380) 631631
Wed 12.00 noon - newer cars
Thur 7.00 pm - part exchange cars
Sat 12.00 noon - general vehicle
auction
Commercial: Every other Thur 6.00 pm

WILTSHIRE

Westbury
Westbury Motor Auctions Ltd
Brook Lane
Westbury
Wilts BA13 4EN
Tel: (01373) 827777
Cars: Tue & Thur 11.00 am
Fri 5.30 pm
Commercials: 1st & 3rd Wed each
*   month 11.00 am*

DORSET

Poole
South Western Vehicle
**   Auctions Ltd**
Kinson Pottery Estate
61 Ringwood Road
Parkstone
Poole
Dorset BH14 0RG
Tel: (01202) 745466
Fax-U-Back: (09003) 416239
Tue 4.30 pm - Cars
Fri 12.30 pm
1st & 3rd Tue of each month
*   4.30 pm - Plant & Commercial*

SOMERSET

Bridgwater
British Car Auctions
Bristol Road (A38)
Bridgwater
Somerset
TA6 4TN
Tel: (01278) 685511
Wed & Fri 10.00 am
MOD: Once every two months
*   Fri 10.00 am*
Motability: Every two weeks
*   Wed 1.00 pm*
Dealer Distribution: Wed 11.00 am
Commercials: Wed 10.00 am

AVON

Bristol
Manheim Auctions
Ashton Vale Road
Ashton Vale
Bristol BS3 2AZ
Tel: (0117) 300 4400
Tue & Thur 10.30 am - cars under
*   5 years old*
Thur 10.30 am - cars over 5 years old
Fleet sales: Tues 10.30 am

DEVON

Exeter
Exeter Car Auctions
Matford Park Road
Marsh Barton
Exeter EX2 8FD
Tel: (01392) 425481
Mon 1.00 pm & Wed 5.00 pm
    Cheaper cars
Mon 1.00 pm Newer Cars
Wed 5.00 pm Cars
1st & 3rd Thur every month
    11.30 am Commercials

CORNWALL

Penryn
Cornwall Motor Auctions
Station Road
Penryn
Cornwall TR10 8HF
Tel: (01326) 372955
Tue & Fri 6.00 pm

CORNWALL contd.

Saltash
Saltash Car Auctions
Gilston Road
Saltash
Cornwall PL12 6TW
Tel: (01752) 841444
Tue 12.00 noon
Thur 6.00 pm

St Austell
South West Motor Auctions
Cattle Market
Pentewan Road
St Austell
Cornwall
Tel: (01726) 70002
Mon 7.00 pm

GLOUCESTERSHIRE

Dursley
Manheim Auctions
Berkley Road (A38)
Cam
Gloucestershire GL11 5JB
Tel: (01453) 542939
Fleet cars: Wed 10.30 am
Older cars, private/trade:
    Sat 11.00 am
4 x 4 Diesel Sale: Wed 10.30 am
    (where stock permits)
Heavy Plant Commercials: Every
    three weeks 1.00 pm Tues
Light Commercials: Every fortnight
    Thur 10.00 am

GLOUCESTERSHIRE contd.

Tewkesbury
British Car Auctions
Newtown Industrial Estate
Northway Lane
Tewkesbury
Gloucestershire GL20 8JG
Tel: (01684) 292307
Cars: Wed & Fri 10.30 am
Light Commercials: Fri 11.00 am
Main Agents Part Exchanges:
  Wed 11.00 am
Fleet/Finance: Fri 12.00 noon
(For specialist titled sales ring for
  details)

HEREFORDSHIRE

Leominster
Leominster Car Auctions Ltd
Kingsland
Nr Leominster
HR6 9RL
Tel: (01568) 708561
Cars: Thur 6.00 pm
Commercials: Thur 8.00 pm
Tools, Accessories, Agricultural
  Machinery and Plant: 2nd Sat
  every month

WEST MIDLANDS

Birmingham
Birmingham Car Auctions Ltd
302-312 Moseley Road
Highgate
Birmingham
B12 0BS
Tel: (0121) 446 4000
Tue & Thur 6.30 pm
Sat 12.00 noon

Birmingham
British Car Auctions
Hayward Industrial Estate
Langley Drive
Chester Road
Birmingham B35 7AD
Tel: (0121) 749 1331
Cars: Mon & Thur 10.30 am
Light Commercials: Wed 2nd &
  4th week 10.30 am
Fleet/Finance: Mon/Thur 10.30 am
(For specialist titled sales ring for
  details)

Coventry
Manheim Auctions
Rowley Drive
Baginton
Coventry
West Midlands CV3 4FG
Tel: (02476) 511150
Franchise Dealers: Ring for details)

WEST MIDLANDS contd.

Darlaston
Manheim Auctions
Whitworth Close
Heath Road
Darlaston
West Midlands WS10 8LJ
Tel: (0121) 568 7500
Mon 5.30 pm, Wed & Fri 10.30 am

Walsall
British Car Auctions
Green Lane
Walsall
West Midlands WS2 7BP
Tel: (01922) 721555
Cars: Tue 10.30 am/Thur 3.30 pm

Wolverhampton
Bowmac Motor Auctions
Dale Street
Bilston
Wolverhampton
West Midlands WV14 7JY
Tel: (01902) 490555
Mon, Wed, Fri 7.00 pm

SHROPSHIRE

Prees Heath
Prees Heath Motor Auction
Heath Road
Whitchurch
Shropshire SY13 2AE
Tel: (01948) 663166/663177
Tue 1.00 pm/Thur 6.30 pm

Telford
Telford Motor Auctions Ltd
Trench Lock 2
Telford
Shropshire
TF1 4FW
Tel: (01952) 257751
Wed 12.00 noon
Fri 6.00 pm

Telford
Telford Car Auctions Ltd
Rookery Road
St Georges
Telford
Shropshire TF2 9BN
Tel: (01952) 610033/4/5
Thur 3.00 pm cars
Every 3rd Sat
Commercial/Plant/Machinery
Sale 1.30 pm

MIDLANDS

Warwick
Warwick Motor Auctions
67 Emscote Road
Warwick
Warwickshire
CV34 5QR
Tel: (01926) 491821
Mon 7.00 pm/Wed 7.00 pm

Leicester
Leicester Car Auctions
8 Commercial Square
Freemans Common Trading Est.
Leicester LE2 7SR
Tel: (01162) 556606
Tue & Thur 6.15 pm

Northampton
NCA National Car Auctions
Salthouse Road
Blackmills Industrial Estate
Northampton NN4 0BD
Tel: (01604) 764041
Tue 5.30 pm
Thur 11.00 am - up to 5 yrs old and
*   more prestigious cars*
Thur 5.00 pm Part exchanges
*   main dealers*

Shepshed
Central Motor Auctions
Charnwood Road
Shepshed
Leicestershire
LE12 9NN
Tel: (01509) 502171
Thur 10.30 am

OXFORDSHIRE

Witney
West Oxfordshire Motor
**   Auctions**
Bromag Industrial Estate
Old A40 Road
Witney
Oxfordshire OX8 7NZ
Tel: (01993) 774413
Tue 6.30 pm
Thur 6.30 pm

BEDFORDSHIRE

Bedford
British Car Auctions
Mile Road
Bedford
MK42 9TB
Tel: (01234) 218161
Cars: Mon 11.00 am/Wed
*   11.00 am/Thur 6.00 pm*
Late Year, Low Mileage:
*   Mon 11.00 am*
Light Commercials: Mon 11.00 am,
*   Thur 6.00 pm*

BUCKINGHAMSHIRE

High Wycombe
Wycombe Auction Centre Ltd
373 Halifax Road
Cressex Industrial Estate
High Wycombe
Bucks HP12 3SD
Tel: (01494) 868690
10.30 am 1st Sat every month

Milton Keynes
Stadium Motor Auctions
Ashland
Milton Keynes
South Bucks MK6 4AA
Tel: (01908) 666835
Wed 6.30 pm/Fri 6.30 pm

CAMBRIDGESHIRE

Peterborough
British Car Auctions
Boongate
Peterborough
Cambs PE1 5AH
Tel: (01733) 568881
*Cars: Mon 4.00 pm/Wed 10.30 am,
  Fri 11.00 am*
*Light Commercials: 10.00 am every
  fortnight*
(For specialist sales ring for details)

NORFOLK

King's Lynn
Anglia Car Auctions
The Cattle Market
Beveridge Way
King's Lynn
Norfolk PE30 4NB
Tel: (01553) 771881
Wed/Fri 6.00 pm

Norwich
East Anglian Motor Auctions Ltd
Auction Centre
261 Aylsham Road
Norwich
NR3 2RE
Tel: (01603) 409824
*Thur 12.00 noon - new cars &
  commercials of all types*
Tue 6.30 pm - older cars, budget

Norwich
Eastern Car Auctions
Norwich Livestock Market
Hall Road
Norwich NR4 6EQ
Tel: (01603) 503037
Thur 6.30 pm
Sat 11.00 am

STAFFORDSHIRE

Stafford
Stafford Motor Auctions
Back Browning Street
Stafford ST16 3AU
Tel: (01785) 243470
Tue & Thur 7.00 pm

Lonton
North Staffordshire Car Auction
Sutherland Road
Lonton
Stoke on Trent
Staffs ST4 2DA
Tel: (01782) 332719
Thur 6.00 pm
Sat 1.00 pm

STAFFORDSHIRE contd.

Measham
British Car Auctions
Tamworth Road
Measham
Swadlincote
Derbyshire DE12 7DY
Tel: (01530) 270322
Cars: Tue 10.30 am & Fri 10.00 am
Light Commercials: Tue 10.00 am
Top Car Sale: 1st Tue at 11.00 am
Heavy Commercials: Alt Fri
*   10.00 am*
4 x 4: 2nd Fri of month,
*   variable - ring for confirmation*
Motability: Alt Tue 12.00 noon

Newcastle (Staffordshire)
Newcastle Motor Auctions
Silverdale Road
Newcastle-under-Lyme
Staffs
Tel: (01782) 617930
Sat 2.00 pm

DERBYSHIRE

Chesterfield
Chesterfield Car Auction
Lockoford Lane
Chesterfield
Derbyshire S41 7JB
Tel: (01246) 277999
Mon/Fri 6.00 pm Wed 1.30 pm

Derby
British Car Auctions
Raynesway
Derby
DE21 7WA
Tel: (01332) 666111
Cars: Mon 3.00 pm
Light Commercials: Alt Thur
*   11.00 am*
Distributor Direct Sale: Mon 3.00 pm
Fleet/Lease Sale: Wed 11.00 am
(For specialist sales ring for details)

LINCOLNSHIRE

Bourne
County Car Auctions Ltd
Eastgate
Bourne
Lincolnshire PE10 9JY
Tel: (01778) 424201
Tue & Thur 6.30 pm

NOTTINGHAMSHIRE

Mansfield
Manheim Car Auction
Fulwood Industrial Estate
Huthwaite
Sutton in Ashfield
Nottinghamshire NG17 6AD
Tel: (01623) 554232
Cars: Tue 11.00 am/Thur 11.00 am
Light Vans: Tue 2.00 pm
Fleet Cars: Tue 11.00 am
Part Exchange Vehicles: Thur 11.00 am

Nottingham
British Car Auctions
Victoria Business Park
Netherfield
Nottingham NG4 2PE
Tel: (0115) 9873311
Cars: Wed/Fri 11.00 am
Light Commercials: 2nd & 4th Fri
*   11.00 am*
Executive/Performance: 3rd Thur
*   11.00 am*
Distribuor: Wed/Fri 12.00 noon
Fleet/Finance: Fri (various times)
(For specialist sales ring for details)

YORKSHIRE

Adwick-Le-Street
Adwick Motor Auctions
Church Lane
Adwick-le-Street
Nr Doncaster DN6 7AY
Tel: (01302) 722251
Tue & Thur 7.00 pm

Bawtry
Bawtry Motor Auction
Corner Garage
Bawtry
Nr Doncaster
South Yorkshire DN10 6JL
Tel: (01302) 710333
Mon/Wed/Fri 7.00 pm

Bradford
Bradford City Motor Auction
Midland Road
Bradford
West Yorkshire BD1 3EQ
Tel: (01274) 774444
Tue & Thur 6.30 pm
Sun 2.00 pm

Bridlington
Bridlington Motor Auctions
Pinfold Lane
Bridlington
East Yorkshire YO16 5XS
Tel: (01262) 674044
Tue & Thur 7.00 pm

YORKSHIRE contd.

Brighouse
British Car Auctions
Armytage Road
Brighouse
Yorkshire HD6 1XE
Tel: (01484) 401555
Cars: Mon & Thur 10.00 am
Top Car Sale: 2nd Thur 12.00 noon
Light Commercials: Fri 10.30 am
Diesel Cars: Last Thur 12.00 noon
4 x 4: 1st Thur 12.00 noon
Late Year, Low Mileage: Thur
  12.30 pm
Fleet & Part Exchanges: Mon/Thur
  10.00 am
Up to £,3000: Tue 6.00 pm
Vans and Commercials:
  Fri 12.00 noon

Knottingley
A1 Motor Auctions
Tadcaster Road
Brotherton
Knottingley
West Yorkshire WS11 9EJ
Tel: (01977) 674151
Tue 1.00 pm
Fri 1.00 pm (over £2,000 reserve)
Tue & Thur 6.00 pm - Cheap cars
  under £2,000 reserve)

173

YORKSHIRE contd.

Leeds
Manheim Auctions
Pontefract Road
Rothwell
Leeds LS26 0JE
Tel: (0870) 4440407
Fleet Cars: Mon/Wed 11.00 am
Cars under £6,000: Wed 11.00 am/
Sat 11.00 am
Heavy Commercials/Plant/
Equipment: Once every three weeks
Thur 10.00 am
Vans & Light Commercials: Mon
11.00 am

Leeds
Motor Auctions Leeds Ltd
Hillidge Road
Leeds
LS10 1DE
Tel: (0113) 277 2644
Mon & Wed: 6.00 pm
Tue & Fri 12.30 pm

Morley
West Riding Motor Auction Ltd
Bruntcliffe Lane
Morley
Leeds
West Yorkshire LS27 9LR
Tel: (0113) 252 1046
Mon/Tue 1.00 pm
Wed/Fri 6.00 pm

YORKSHIRE contd.

Rotherham
Manheim Auctions
West Bawtry Road
Canklow Meadows Industrial Est.
Rotherham
South Yorkshire S60 2XL
Tel: (01709) 378989
Wed 11.00 am/Fri 10.30 am

MANCHESTER AND MERSEYSIDE

Chester
Direct Motor Auctions
Unit 9 Hartford Way
Sealand Industrial Estate
Chester CH1 4NT
Tel: (01244) 383789
Mon/Wed 6.30 pm
Sat 12.30 pm

Ellesmere Port
Ellesmere Port Motor Auction
Rossfield Road
Rossmore Industrial Estate
Ellesmere Port
South Wirral CH65 3BS
Tel: (0151) 357 2040
Mon & Fri 7.00 pm
Thur 2.30 pm
Commercial: Last Mon every month
6.30 pm

MANCHESTER AND MERSEYSIDE contd.

Haydock
Manheim Auctions
Yewtree Trading Estate
Kilbuck Lane
Haydock
Merseyside WA11 9SZ
Tel: (01942) 721245
Cars: Wed 6.00 pm/Fri 10.30 am
Light Commercials: 2nd & 4th Tue
*   of the month 11.00 am*
Fleet: Fri 10.30 am

Manchester
British Car Auctions
Red Gate Lane
Belle Vue
Manchester M12 4RX
Tel: (0161) 230 6000
Cars: Tue 10.30 am/Fri 10.30 am
Light Commercials: Wed 11.00 am
Heavy Commercials: Alternate Wed
*   10.00 am*
Late Year, Low Mileage:
*   Tue 1.30 pm*
4 x 4/Diesel Cars: 2nd Tue
*   12.00 noon*
Fleet/Finance: Tue/Fri 11.00 am

MANCHESTER AND MERSEYSIDE contd.

Radcliffe
Radcliffe & District Motor
**   Auction**
Unit 7 Globe Industrial Estate
Spring Lane
Radcliffe
Nr Bolton
Greater Manchester
M26 2TA
Tel: (0161) 724 0805
Mon/Wed/Fri 7.00 pm

Manchester
Stoodley Vehicle Auctions
Hyde Road
Belle Vue
Manchester
M12 4SA
Tel: (0161) 223 3882
Cars: Mon & Wed 6.00 pm/Sat
*   12 noon*
Light Commercials/Cars: Fri 3.30 pm
Plant & Equipment: 2nd Tue of
*   every month 1.00 pm*

Manchester
Manheim Auctions
Pilkington House
Richmond Road
Trafford Park
Manchester M17 1RE
Tel: (0161) 872 0655
Cars: Tue & Thur 6.00 pm
Fleet: Thur 11.00 am

MANCHESTER AND MERSEYSIDE contd.

Liverpool

Liverpool Motor Auctions
Dorset House
West Derby Road
Liverpool L6 4BR
Tel: (0151) 263 7351
Mon 6.00 pm/Wed 3.00pm/
Fri 4.00 pm

St Helens

St Helens Motor Auctions
East Lancs Road
Carr Mill
St Helens
Merseyside WA11 9LG
Tel: (01744) 22513
Mon & Wed 7.00 pm

LANCASHIRE

Blackpool

West Coast Motor Auctions Ltd
Wyrefields
Poulton Industrial Estate
Poulton Le Fylde
Blackpool FY6 8JF
Tel: (01253) 892488
Mon & Wed 7.00 pm

Blackburn

East Lancs Motor Auctions
Highfield Road
(off Bolton Road)
Blackburn
Lancs
BB2 3RE
Tel: (01254) 670190
Tue/Thur 7.00 pm

Burnley

Burnley Motor Auctions
Liverpool Road
Rosegrove
Burnley
Lancs BB12 6HH
Tel: (01282) 427231
Mon/Thur 7.15 pm
Every 3rd Sat: Plant & Commercial
Vehicles 10.00 am
(ring for details)

Chorley

Chorley Motor Auction
Cottam Street
off Pall Mall
Chorley
Lancs PR7 2DT
Tel: (01257) 262091
Tue & Fri 8.00 pm

LANCASHIRE contd.

Preston
Olympia Motor Auction Ltd
London Road
Preston
Lancs PR2 5AN
Tel: (01772) 253230
Mon/Thur 7.15 pm

Preston
British Car Auctions
Reedfield Place
Walton Summit
Preston
Lancs PR5 8AA
Tel: (01772) 324666
Cars: Mon & Wed 10.30 am
Light Commercials: Every Thur of the
month 11.00 am
Motability: Every other Wed 12.00
noon
(For specialist sales ring for details)

CUMBRIA

Carlisle
Borderway Motor Auctions
Montgomery Way
Rosehill Industrial Estate
Carlisle
Cumbria CA1 2RW
Tel: (01228) 590990
Tue 11.00 am
Fri 1.00 pm
2nd Sat every month 11.00 am

CO. DURHAM

Birtley
Scottish Motor Auction
Portobello Industrial Estate
Birtley
Chester-le-Street
Co. Durham
Tel: (0191) 410 4243/9447
Cars: Mon/Wed 7.00 pm
Fri 1.00 pm
Commercials: Fri 12.00 noon
HGV/Plant: 1st Fri 11.30 am
Small Plant/Equipment: 1st Fri
11.30 am

Ferryhill
Durham County Motor Auctions
Mainsforth Industrial Estate
Ferryhill
Co. Durham
DL17 9DE
Tel: (01740) 650065
Tue & Thur 6.00 pm
Thur 11.00 am (over £2,000)

177

CO. DURHAM contd.

Maltby
Manheim Auctions
Low Road
Maltby
Middlesbrough
TS8 0BW
Tel: (01642) 760363
Mon/Wed 6.00 pm
*   Cars under £2,000*
Thur/Fri 11.00 am
*   Cars over £2,000*

TYNE & WEAR

Newcastle upon Tyne
British Car Auctions
Whitley Road
Longbenton
Newcastle upon Tyne
Tyne & Wear NE12 9SQ
Tel: (0191) 270 0077
Cars: Tue/Thur 12.00 noon
Fleet Cars: Tue/Thur 12.00 noon
Motability: Twice per month,
*   Tue 1.30 pm*
Light Commercials: Every other Tue
*   12.00 noon*
Heavy Commercials: Last Tue of
*   month 12.00 noon*
(For specialist sales ring for details)

TYNE & WEAR contd.

North Shields
Tyne Tees Motor Auction Ltd
Coast Road Retail Park
Coast Road (A1058)
North Shields
Tyne & Wear NE29 7UJ
Tel: (0191) 296 2020
Mon 2.00 pm
Wed 5.30 pm
Fri 4.30 pm
Fleet: Wed 1.00 pm

Washington
Manheim Auctions
District 15
Pattinson Road
Washington
Tyne & Wear NE38 8LB
Tel: (0191) 419 0000
Cars: Sat 11.00 am
*   Wed Fri 11.00 am Thur 6.00 pm*
Fleet Cars: Wed/Fri 11.00 am
Light Commercials: Wed 12.00 noon
Commercials & Plant: 3rd Tue
*   11.00 am*

SCOTLAND

Aberdeen
Thainstone Vehicle Auctions
Thainstone Centre
Inverurie
Aberdeen AB51 5XZ
Tel: (01467) 623700
Mon/Thur 6.00 pm
1st Mon of month, 6.00 pm
   Light Commercial

Aberdeen
Scottish Motor Auction Group
11 St Machar Road
Aberdeen AB24 2UU
Tel: (01224) 487000
Mon/Thur 7.00 pm

Edinburgh
British Car Auctions
Edinburgh Exhibition & Trade
   Centre
Ingliston
Ingliston Road
Newbridge
Edinburgh EH28 8NB
Tel: (0131) 333 2151
Cars: Mon/Thur 11.00 am
   Tue 6.00 pm
Top Car Sale: 3rd Thur 2.30 pm
(For specialist sales ring for details)

SCOTLAND contd.

Edinburgh
Scottish Motor Auction Group
1 Murrayburn Road
Longstone
Edinburgh EH14 2TF
Tel: (0131) 443 7163
Mon & Thur 6.30 pm

Glasgow
Central Car Auctions
33 Scotland Street
Glasgow G5 8NB
Tel: (0141) 429 1011
Wed 1.00 pm
Fri 6.30 pm

Glasgow
ADT Auctions
999 Royston Road
Glasgow G21 2AA
Tel: (0141) 770 9661
Cars: Wed/Fri 11.00 am
   Mon 6.00 pm
Late Year, Low Mileage: Every Wed
   12.00 noon
(For specialist sales ring for details)

179

SCOTLAND contd.

Intercity Motor Auctions Ltd
77 Melbourne Street
Glasgow G31 1BQ
Tel: (0141) 556 3333
Wed 12.30 pm
Thur 6.00 pm
Sun 1.00 pm

Kinross
Scottish Motor Auction Group
Brigend
Kinross KY13 7EN
Tel: (01577) 862564
Mon/Wed/Fri 6.30 pm
Cars & Commercials: 11.30 am
*   last Fri in month*

Lanarkshire
Shotts Motor Auction
Stane Road
Shotts
Lanarkshire ML7 5NH
Tel: (01501) 823337
Tue 12.00 noon
Thur 6.00 pm
(More commercials on Tue)

Strathclyde
British Car Auctions
Main Street
Newmains
Wishaw
Strathclyde ML2 9PT
Tel: (01698) 383737
Cars: Tue 11.00 am/Wed 6.00 pm
Light Commercials: Thur 11.00 am
Heavy Commercials: Last Thur of
*   month 10.00 am*
(For specialist sales ring for details)

SCOTLAND contd.

Glasgow
Manheim Auctions
Siemen Street
Blochairn
Glasgow G21 2BU
Tel: (0141) 553 4747
Tue 6.30 pm
Fri 4.30 pm
Fleet Sales: 1st & 3rd Tue
*   12.00 noon*
Commercial Sales: 2nd Fri 11.00 am

Tayside
Forfar Auctions Trading Co Ltd
Carseview Road
Forfar
Angus DD8 3BT
Tel: (01307) 462197
Tue 6.30 pm

WALES

Anglesey
Gwynedd Motor Auctions
Gaerwen
Anglesey
North Wales LL60 6DF
Tel: (01248) 723303
1st Thur of every month 6.00 pm

Cardiff
British Car Auctions
Meadows Road
Queensway Meadows Ind. Est.
Newport
Gwent NP9 0YR
Tel: (01633) 270222
Cars: Mon/Thur 10.30 am
Light Commercials: Mon 10.00 am
Plant: Once a month on Tue
*   10.00 am*
Fleet/Finance: Mon 11.00 am
Dealer/Distributor: Thur 11.30 am
Late Year/Low Mileage: Thur
*   12.00 noon*

WALES contd.

Deeside
Clwyd Car Auctions
Holywell Road
Ewloe
Deeside
Clwyd CH5 3BS
Tel: (01244) 532821/532996
Wed & Sat 2.00 pm
1st Mon every month 5.00 pm -
*   Commercials*
2nd Mon every month 6.00 pm -
*   Plant*

Merthyr Tydfil
Merthyr Motor Auctions
Pant Road
Dowlais
Merthyr Tydfil
Mid Glam. CF48 3SH
Tel: (01685) 377818
Mon 5.30 pm/Wed 6.30 pm/
*   Sat 2.00 pm*

Newport
Newport Motor Auctions Ltd
Dockland Distributor Road
Newport
Gwent NP20 2BX
Tel: (01633) 215853/256380
Mon, Wed & Fri 7.00 pm

Queensferry (Clwyd)
Queensferry TMA Ltd
Station Road
Queensferry
Deeside
Clwyd CH5 2TD
Tel: (01244) 812811
Tue 6.00 pm
Fri 1.00 pm

WALES contd.

Swansea
Swansea Motor Vehicle Auctions
Riverside Yard
Neath Road
Briton Ferry
SA11 2NL
Tel: (01639) 814899
Wed 6.00 pm/Sat 11.00 am

N. IRELAND

Ballyclare
Ballyclare Motor Auction
53 Park Street
Ballyclare
Co. Antrim
N. Ireland BT39 9DQ
Tel: (02893) 352557
Wed 7.00 pm

Belfast
**Carryduff Car & Commercial
    Auction**
10 Comber Road
Carryduff
Belfast
Co. Down
N. Ireland BT8 8AN
Tel: (02890) 813775
Mon 6.30 pm/Wed 7.00 pm
Every other Sat 10.00 am -
    Commercial Vehicles

Newtownabbey
Wilsons Auctions Ltd
22 Mallusk Road
Glengormley
Newtownabbey BT36 4PP
Tel: (02890) 342626
Tue & Thur 7.00 pm

N. IRELAND contd.

Omagh
Omagh Auction Centre
Unit 24 Gortrush Industrial
    Estate
Omagh
Co.Tyrone
BT78 5EJ
Tel: (02882) 241514
Mon/Thur 7.30 pm

Portadown
Wilsons Auctions Ltd
65 Seagoe Industrial Estate
Portadown BT63 5QE
Tel: (02838) 336433
Wed 6.30 pm/Sat 11.30 am

CHAPTER TWENTY ONE

Manufacturers and Importers

ALFA ROMEO - See FIAT AUTO ALFA ROMEO LTD.

ASTON MARTIN LAGONDA LTD, Tickford Street, Newport Pagnell, Buckinghamshire MK 16 9AN (01908) 610620.

AUDI - See VOLKSWAGEN GROUP UK.

BENTLEY - See ROLLS-ROYCE & BENTLEY MOTOR CARS LTD.

BMW (GB) LTD, Ellesfield Avenue, Bracknell, Berkshire RG12 8TA (01344) 426565.

BRISTOL CARS LTD, 368-370 Kensington High Street, London W14 8NL (0207) 603 5556.

CHRYSLER - See DAIMLER CHRYSLER.

CITROEN UK LTD, 221 Bath Road, Slough, Berkshire SL1 4BA (08706) 069000.

DAIHATSU VEHICLE DISTRIBUTORS LTD, Ryder Street, West Bromwich, West Midlands B70 0EJ (01215) 205000.

DAIMLER CHRYSLER UK LTD, Tongwell, Milton Keynes MK15 8BA (01908) 301000.

DAIMLER JAGUAR - See JAGUAR CARS LTD.

DE TOMASO, Emila Concessionaires Ltd, Unit 15 Silverstone Circuit, Northants NN12 8TL (01327) 857880.

FERRARI & MASERATI UK, Thorpe Industrial Estate, Ten Acre Lane, Egham, Surrey TW20 8RJ (01784) 436222.

FIAT AUTO ALFA ROMEO LTD, Fiat House, 266 Bath Road, Slough, Berkshire SL1 4HJ (01753) 511431.

FORD MOTOR CO LTD, Eagle Way, Brentwood, Essex CM13 3BW (01277) 253000.

HONDA (UK) LTD, 470 London Road, Slough, Berkshire SL3 8QY (01753) 590500.

HYUNDAI CARS (UK) LTD, St John's Court, Easton Street, High Wycombe, Buckinghamshire HP11 1JX (01494) 428600.

ISUZU (UK) LTD, Ryder Street, Great Bridge, West Bromwich, West Midlands B70 0EJ (0121) 522 2000.

JAGUAR CARS LTD, Browns Lane, Allesley, Coventry, West Midlands CV5 9DR (02476) 402121.

JEEP - See DAIMLER CHRYSLER LTD.

KIA (UK) LTD, 77 Mount Ephraim, Tunbridge Wells, Kent TN4 8BS (01892) 513454.

LADA CARS, Motor Vehicle Industries, PO Box 1, Carnaby Industrial Estate, Carnaby, Bridlington YO15 3QX (01262) 402200.

LAMBORGHINI, Lamborghini London, Melton Court, 27 Old Brompton, London SW7 3TD (0207) 5891472.

LANCIA (UK) LTD, See FIAT AUTO ALFA ROMEO LTD.

LAND ROVER LTD, Lode Lane, Solihull, West Midlands B92 8NW (0121) 722 2424.

LEXUS - See TOYOTA (GB) LTD.

LOTUS CARS LTD, Hethel, Norwich, Norfolk NR14 8EZ (01953) 608000.

MARCOS SALES LTD, 153 West Wilts Trading Estate, Westbury, Wiltshire BA13 4JN (01373) 864097.

MAZDA CARS (UK) LTD, 77 Mount Ephraim, Tunbridge Wells, Kent TN4 8BS (01892) 511877.

MERCEDES BENZ - See DAIMLER CHYRSLER UK LTD.

MITSUBISHI MOTORS LTD, Watermoor, Cirencester, Gloucestershire GL7 1LF (1285) 655777.

MORGAN MOTOR CO. LTD, Pickersleigh Road, Malvern Link, Worcestershire WR14 2LL (01684) 573104.

NISSAN MOTOR (GB) LTD, The Rivers Office Park, Denham Way, Rickmansworth, Hertfordshire WD3 9YS (01923) 899999.

PEUGEOT MOTOR CO. PLC, Aldermoor House, PO Box 227, Aldermoor Lane, Coventry, West Midlands CV3 1LT (02476) 884000.

PORSCHE CARS GREAT BRITAIN LTD, Bath Road, Calcot, Reading, Berkshire RG31 7SE (0118) 9303666.

PROTON CARS (UK) LTD, Proton House, Marsh Lane, Royal Portbury Dock, Bristol, Avon BS20 0PN (01275) 375475.

RANGE ROVER - See LAND ROVER LTD.

RENAULT (UK) LTD, The Rivers Office Park, Denham Way, Maple Cross, Rickmansworth, Hertfordshire WD3 9YS (01793) 486001.

RELIANT MOTORS LTD, Off Kennock Road, Burntwood, Staffordshire WS7 8GB (01543) 459222.

ROCSTA, Asia Motors (UK) Ltd, 77 Mount Ephraim, Tunbridge Wells, Kent TN4 8BS (01892) 513454.

ROLLS-ROYCE & BENTLEY MOTOR CARS LTD, Pyms Lane, Crewe, Cheshire CW1 3PL (01270) 255155.

MG ROVER GROUP LTD, PO Box 41, Longbridge, Birmingham B31 2TB (0121) 475 2101.

SAAB (GB) LTD, Saab House, Globe Park, Marlow, Buckinghamshire SL7 1LY (01628) 486977.

SEAT (UK) LTD, Delaware Drive, Blakelands, Milton Keynes MK14 5AN (01908) 261444.

SKODA UK, Yeomans Drive, Blakelands, Milton Keynes MK14 5AN (01908) 264000.

SUBARU (UK) LTD, Ryder Street, West Bromwich, West Midlands B70 0EJ (0121) 522 2000.

SUZUKI GB PLC, 46-62 Gatwick Road, Crawley, West Sussex RH10 2XF (01293) 518000.

TOYOTA (GB) LTD, The Quadrangle, Redhill, Surrey RH1 1PX (01737) 768585.

TVR ENGINEERING LTD, Bristol Avenue, Blackpool,
Lancashire FY2 0JF (01253) 356151.

VAUXHALL MOTORS LTD, Griffin House, Osborne Road,
Luton, Bedfordshire LU1 3YT (01582) 427200.

VOLVO CAR (UK) LTD, Globe Park, Marlow, Buckinghamshire
SL7 1YQ (01628) 477977.

VOLKSWAGEN GROUP UK, Yeomans Drive, Blakelands, Milton
Keynes MK14 5AN (01908) 679121.

REGISTRATION LETTERS SUFFIX

Suffix Letters

Registrations ending with letters

A	Feb 1963 to Dec 1963
B	Jan 1964 to Dec 1964
C	Jan 1965 to Dec 1965
D	Jan 1966 to Dec 1966
E	Jan 1967 to July 1967
F	Aug 1967 to July 1968
G	Aug 1968 to July 1969
H	Aug 1969 to July 1970
J	Aug 1970 to July 1971
K	Aug 1971 to July 1972
L	Aug 1972 to July 1973
M	Aug 1973 to July 1974
N	Aug 1974 to July 1975
P	Aug 1975 to July 1976
R	Aug 1976 to July 1977
S	Aug 1977 to July 1978
T	Aug 1978 to July 1979
V	Aug 1979 to July 1980
W	Aug 1980 to July 1981
X	Aug 1981 to July 1982
Y	Aug 1982 to July 1983

REGISTRATION LETTERS PREFIX

Prefix Letters

Registrations beginning with letters

A	Aug 1983 to July 1984
B	Aug 1984 to July 1985
C	Aug 1985 to July 1986
D	Aug 1986 to July 1987
E	Aug 1987 to July 1988
F	Aug 1988 to July 1989
G	Aug 1989 to July 1990
H	Aug 1990 to July 1991
J	Aug 1991 to July 1992
K	Aug 1992 to July 1993
L	Aug 1993 to July 1994
M	Aug 1994 to July 1995
N	Aug 1995 to July 1996
P	Aug 1996 to July 1997
R	Aug 1997 to July 1998
S	Aug 1998 to Feb 1999
T	March 1999
V	September 1999
W	March 2000
X	September 2000
Y	March 2001

That concludes this edition of *Four Wheels to a Fortune.* I hope you have enjoyed it and, on behalf of myself and the publishers, may I wish you good luck and best wishes for a lucrative future!

Printed in Great Britain
by Amazon

85046618R00108